JOHN OSBORNE

WORLD DRAMATISTS SERIES

First Titles

Edward Albee	*Ronald Hayman*
Anton Chekhov	*Siegfried Melchinger*
Henrik Ibsen	*Hans Georg Meyer*
John Osborne	*Ronald Hayman*
Arthur Miller	*Ronald Hayman*
Arthur Schnitzler	*Reinhard Urbach*
August Strindberg	*Gunnar Ollén*
Arnold Wesker	*Ronald Hayman*

WORLD DRAMATISTS

JOHN OSBORNE

RONALD HAYMAN

With halftone illustrations

FREDERICK UNGAR PUBLISHING CO.
NEW YORK

First American publication 1972

© 1968, 1969, 1972 by Ronald Hayman
Printed in the United States of America
Library of Congress Catalog Card Number: 79-153123
Designed by Edith Fowler
  ISBN 0-8044-2386-5 (cloth)

ACKNOWLEDGMENTS

The author would like to thank Catherine Barton, Martha Crewe, John Peter, Charles Tomlinson, and Irving Wardle for their help in reading manuscripts and making useful comments when the series was in preparation.

The author and publishers wish to thank the following for permission to include quotations from the publications listed below:

Look Back in Anger: John Osborne and Faber & Faber Ltd; *Epitaph for George Dillon, The Entertainer, The World of Paul Slickey, A Subject of Scandal and Concern, Luther, The Blood of the Bambergs, Under Plain Cover, Inadmissible Evidence, A Patriot for Me, A Bond Honoured, Time Present, The Hotel in Amsterdam:* John Osborne and David Higham Associates, Ltd; *Declaration:* John Osborne, MacGibbon & Kee Ltd and David Higham Associates, Ltd; *West of Suez:* John Osborne, Faber and Faber, Ltd, and David Higham Associates, Ltd.

CONTENTS

CHRONOLOGY

1929 Born in London on December 12th of Anglo-Welsh parents.

1941 Death of father. Insurance money is used to send Osborne, who had failed the grammar school entrance examination, to Belmont College, Devon.

1944 Expelled from school after slapping the director, he goes to work as a trade journalist.

1945 Starts working as an actor in provincial repertory and tour companies.

1949 His first attempt at playwriting, *The Devil Inside,* produced at the Theatre Royal, Huddersfield.

1951 Marries actress Pamela Lane.

1953 Collaborates with Canadian actor-playwright Anthony Creighton on *Personal Enemy,* which is produced at Harrogate.

1956 Joins London's Royal Court Theatre and acts in Ronald Duncan's *Don Juan,* Nigel Dennis's *Cards of Identity,* Bertolt Brecht's *The Good Woman of Setzuan,* and Jean Giraudoux's *The Apollo of Bellac.* The production of *Look Back in Anger* immediately establishes his reputation as a leading playwright.

1957 Forms Woodfall Film Productions with director Tony Richardson. Divorces Pamela Lane and marries actress Mary Ure. Sir Laurence Olivier commissions *The Entertainer*.

1959   Film version of *Look Back in Anger*.

1960   Film version of *The Entertainer*.

1962   Writes the film script for Tony Richardson's *Tom Jones*.

1963   Divorces Mary Ure and marries film critic Penelope Gilliatt.

1965   Directs Charles Wood's *Meals on Wheels* at the Royal Court Theatre.

1966   Completes film script of *The Charge of the Light Brigade*.

1968   Divorces Penelope Gilliatt and marries actress Jill Bennett.

INTRODUCTION:
JOHN OSBORNE

At times of almost revolutionary change, such as have been seen in the English theater since the war, the drama critic has to join in the fight. The best theater criticism of the last twenty years, like Kenneth Tynan's pieces in *The Observer* and some of the articles in *Encore*, was detached enough to be critical of the new movement, but they were also part of it, currents in the tide. Today it's no longer necessary to go on fighting a battle that's been won. The time has come to take stock of the ground that's been gained and above all to be objective about assessing the achievements of individual playwrights and individual plays. We can concede that some of the Kitchen Sink plays have been just as sentimental and inaccurate about the working classes as their predecessors were about the aristocracy, and we can see that many of the writers who seemed so full of promise, like Shelagh Delaney and N. F. Simpson, have failed to develop into playwrights of much importance.

The four most important talents to emerge in the middle fifties were Samuel Beckett, John Osborne,

Harold Pinter, and John Arden, and, of the four, Osborne was the one who had the most direct influence
on the new movement. He was also the one who was
most explicitly concerned with class, and, as in all
revolutions, class has been a very important factor.
The working classes that had been banging at the
door for so long have been let in. The West End
audience is still primarily middle-class and the commercial West End theater is still thoroughly middle-
class in its structure, but a new pattern is emerging
in the subsidized noncommercial theaters that present their plays in repertoire. What the Royal Shakespeare Theatre and the National Theatre are doing is
very different from what used to be done at Stratford-
on-Avon and the Old Vic. Ensemble theater has ar-
rived in England at last and is already changing the
whole complexion of the English theater. This is
largely due to Brecht and the Berliner Ensemble, and
to Joan Littlewood and Kenneth Tynan, who in their
different ways have been fighting for it for the best
part of twenty years. Joan Littlewood's pioneering at
Stratford East prepared the ground for the Royal
Court and the Royal Court (which was subsidized
more by Osborne's films than it was by the Arts
Council) prepared the ground for the ensemble theater of today.

What I mean by the ensemble theater is illustrated
by Peter Hall's and John Barton's 1963 production
of *The Wars of the Roses* and the next year's production of *Henry IV, Parts I and II* by John Barton,
Trevor Nunn, and Clifford Williams. The possibility
of two or three directors collaborating on one production would have seemed unlikely in England ten
years earlier, though it was common practice in the
Berliner Ensemble. But it was only in 1960 that Peter
Hall introduced the idea of long-term contracts

for actors. The stability this provides both in the actor's life and in the company is a basic prerequisite for the growth of team spirit in a group of actors and for the style of production and acting that has evolved. The Royal Shakespeare Company has also followed the example of the Berliner Ensemble in starting a studio for members of the company to work at voice production, singing, movement and acting exercises; however, partly because of financial difficulties, studio activities have sometimes had to be suspended.

The resultant style is a style of Shakespearean production which is quite new in England but which derives (legitimately) very largely from Brecht. It is an antiheroic style with a great deal of emphasis on the ordinary facts of the ordinary life of the ordinary man. The soldiers are not just extras who compose into a decorative group: they are presented as men who pant and sweat, who get thirsty and tired as they drag their baggage and their carts around. Their weapons are realistic, the heavy texture of their costumes is realistic, and the mud, blood and scars are realistic. Stage business is no longer a series of illustrative flourishes, an unimportant accompaniment to the poetry and the speechmaking: it is central to the conception of the production.

A great deal depends on the designer, and John Bury of the Royal Shakespeare Company—he was formerly Joan Littlewood's designer—owes an incalculable debt to Brecht and to Brecht's designers, like Caspar Neher. This was also true of Jocelyn Herbert at the Royal Court. There is the same sparseness of décor, the same use of subfusc colors and white light, and the same reliance on solid foreground objects like wagons and council tables to create the atmosphere of each locale.

I think these Shakespearean productions are representative of a new trend that is already becoming important in the English theater. The extent to which the commercial theater in London and in the provinces can imitate the heavily subsidized National Theatre and the Royal Shakespeare Theatre is obviously limited. They cannot afford such large casts, or operate an ensemble system, and they're more dependent on the box-office appeal of star names. But in both design and direction, there has been a very big swing towards the ensemble style and the clearest gauge of the reorientation of the whole English theater is in the new approach to casting. Fashions have changed so completely that people forget what preconceptions were in the fifties on what an actor ought to look like and sound like. Gritty provincial accents have outnumbered educated R.A.D.A. (Royal Academy of Dramatic Art) voices, and even conventional good looks are getting rarer among the fashionable faces of today. When Arthur Miller was in England for the production of *A View from the Bridge*, he complained how hard it was to find English actors who could play "common man" parts. Today it's harder to find young actors who can be convincing as princes or aristocrats. By casting actors like David Warner and Ian Holm as princes, Peter Hall has started a new convention of putting the emphasis on what Shakespeare's royal heroes have in common with the common man, not on what differentiates them from him.

What has John Osborne's place been in this vast swing of fashion? The journalists who talk about a "revolution" in the English theater date its beginning on May 8, 1956, when *Look Back in Anger* opened at the Royal Court. Obviously it wasn't a revolution that happened overnight but Osborne did more than anyone to popularize the new type of hero and the new type of actor. In fact it's quite difficult to see how Albert Finney, Peter O'Toole, Nicol Williamson, Richard Harris, Tom Courtenay, and Robert Stephens could have achieved the success they have if Kenneth Haigh hadn't blazed the trail with the first of the "angry" young heroes.

Not that *anger* is really the right word. Osborne used it in his title and "angry young man" stayed in fashion as a catchphrase for a long time, but anger has to be directed against something and if you're angry about everything, then you're not really angry. Jimmy Porter pours the same sulphuric energy into the attacks he launches on everything that surrounds him—Alison, Cliff, Helena, the Sunday papers, the social system, women in general, Conservative Members of Parliament, Sunday cinema audiences, Billy Graham, the H-Bomb, people who don't like jazz, phony politeness, nostalgia for the imperial past, Wordsworth, Alison's mother, people who have never watched anyone dying, the Church, and the apathy of everyone else in a generation that scarcely has anything to be positive about. Jimmy is himself negative in that he has no alternatives to offer. He'd like to see things changed but he has no ideas about what they ought to be changed to. Osborne is no latter-day Shaw with a program of social reforms. His basic feeling seems to be that if there aren't any "good brave causes" left that are worth dying for, then there can't be any causes that are worth fighting for. This is a romantic and very negative assumption but Osborne managed to lend a positive ring to it and one of the main reasons for Jimmy Porter's popularity was his success as an embodiment of the man of action who was frustrated because there was nothing he could go into action for. It was very comfortable to identify with him on this score

and thousands of people have taken him to their
hearts who in ordinary life would find such a man
boorish, arrogant and tiresome. But they forgave him
because he made disaffection sound like a credo and
because he revamped apathy into a wildly spirited
aggression that hit out at everything, including
apathy.

> Nobody can be bothered. No one can raise them-
> selves out of their delicious sloth . . . Oh heavens,
> how I long for a little ordinary human enthusiasm.
> Just enthusiasm—that's all. I want to hear a warm
> thrilling voice cry out Hallelujah! Hallelujah! I'm
> alive! I've an idea. Why don't we have a little
> game? Let's pretend that we're human beings, and
> that we're actually alive. Just for a while. What do
> you say? Let's pretend we're human. *(He looks
> from one to the other.)* Oh, brother, it's such a long
> time since I was with anyone who got enthusiastic
> about anything.

Jimmy fights on the only two battlefields that he
sees as being available to him: sex and talk. In the
sexual episodes, Osborne uses Jimmy very much like
a conventional character in a conventional play; in
the speechmaking, he doesn't. The action never altogether comes to a stop while Jimmy is talking and
the fact that the long monologues get so many laughs
helps enormously in keeping the play buoyant, but
Osborne isn't just telling a story about a character
called Jimmy Porter. He is using the stage as a plat-
form and the character as a mouthpiece for a large
mixture of points that he badly wants to make. Most
of them are aimed against the Establishment.

> Well, you've never heard so many well-bred com-
> monplaces come from beneath the same bowler hat.
> The Platitude from Outer Space—that's brother
> Nigel. He'll end up in the Cabinet one day, make

else's indifference. Bill is an ordinary professional man, a solicitor, whose life starts to follow the pattern of his anxiety dream, which is that he's been summoned to justify his existence in front of a court made up of his employees. In the dream sequence we see him in the dock trying to defend himself and failing to put the words together into a coherent statement. In the office sequences that follow we see him using arguments and persuasions in a very similar way, trying and failing to convince the people around him that they need him. But he knows how desperately he needs them. One by one we see them drawing away from him, his office girls, his clerks, his clients, his daughter, his girl friend, until he's forced to a final awareness of being alone with himself. And if no one needs you, no one wants to work for you or sleep with you or consult you or even speak to you over the telephone, then you find out that all you've ever had is yourself. And what if that isn't enough? The play makes compulsive theater because it's like a relentless game of strip poker, played out with social, family, professional and sexual relationships, ending up in a naked isolation which is worse than the nightmare.

The theme of isolation (especially growing isolation) has been very important in Osborne's work. In spite of the contact he makes with Cliff and Alison and Helena, Jimmy Porter is presented as being very much alone in his suffering awareness of what's wrong with everything. In some respects he's a development of the hero of *Epitaph for George Dillon*, Osborne's first professional play, which he wrote in collaboration with Anthony Creighton. George becomes, in effect, a member of an ordinary suburban family, but everything about him sets him apart from everyone else—his "artistic temperament," his vulnerable sensitivity, the level of his awareness, even his tuberculosis. In Osborne's television play, *A Subject of Scandal and Concern*, George Holyoake stands completely alone because of his integrity and his refusal to compromise with a society that equates atheism with blasphemy. Luther is a revolutionary who stands out against the Church, the Emperor, and all the pressures that a conformist century can put on him to conform. Redl in *A Patriot for Me* is presented as the truest kind of patriot—the man who's willing to betray his country out of loyalty to his real self. And Osborne himself, in his notorious letter to *Tribune*, bravely (if neurotically) fired a furious salvo against everyone and everything in England.

> My hatred for you is almost the only constant satisfaction you have left me. My favourite fantasy is four minutes or so non-commercial viewing as you fry in your democratically elected hot-seats in Westminster, preferably with your condoning democratic constituents.

> There is murder in my brain, and I carry a knife in my heart for every one of you. Macmillan, and you, Gaitskell, you particularly. I wish we could hang you all out, with your dirty washing, on your damned Oder-Neisse line, and those seven out of ten Americans too. I would willingly watch you all die for the West, if only I could keep my own minuscule portion of it, you could all go ahead —die for Berlin, for Democracy, to keep out the Red hordes or whatever you like.

> You have instructed me in my hatred for thirty years. You have perfected it, and made it the blunt, obsolete instrument it is now. I only hope it will keep me going. I think it will. I think it may sustain me in the last few months.

> Till then, damn you, England. You're rotting now—quite soon you'll disappear.

Osborne is in love with the image of one man fighting single-handed against his country or his century, but not very interested in the issues that make the fight necessary. In his own letter, as in Jimmy Porter's tirades or Bill Maitland's long speech to his daughter, the mood of disgust is clear and the gesture of rejection is clear but the reasons for them are anything but clear. His *Luther* is a play about a rebel but it's only very perfunctorily concerned with indulgences and justification by faith, and scarcely concerned at all with other questions of dogma or of abuses in the Church. He presents the rebellion without bothering too much about the reasons for it.

This is why he writes so much in terms of monologue and this is why the heroes always outgrow the structures of the plays that contain them. They're always full of fighting spirit but they're not at all sure what they're fighting for. What they're fighting against is neither limited to nor defined by the incidents and relationships that make up the action, and while the mouthpiece monologues dictate the rhythm and shape of the whole play, as they do, it's impossible for the spokesman-hero to be put into any sort of critical perspective. We see his world (which is very much our world) through his eyes and through his attacks on it, but we can't see him as part of the world that he's living in. In Shakespeare, even a towering egomaniac like Lear is contained by the world of the play and is therefore capable of being altered by other elements inside it. At the end of the play he's lost everything he ever had, but gained the ability to see himself as other people see him. None of Osborne's heroes can ever do that because they're all written from inside the egomania. They're designed to communicate with the audience directly, rather than through give-and-take with the other

characters in the play, who are seldom allowed to
exist on the same level of reality as they do.

This preferential treatment of heroes who tend to
isolate themselves from society is a strange feature to
find in a writer of professed left-wing leanings. Altogether, Osborne seems oddly intent on the One and
indifferent to the Many. Most of his heroes come
from the working class, but none of them are representative of it and none of them are ever seen against
a working-class background. A few of the minor
characters are typically working-class, like Cliff and
Luther's father, and there are signs of a good deal
of affection for the typical working-class mother.
Phoebe Rice is the only one who actually makes an
appearance but Luther's mother is mentioned and
Jimmy Porter often refers very warmly to Hugh's
mum, who is a charwoman. The hero of *The World
of Paul Slickey* is also the son of an off-stage charwoman. But affection for working-class people is one
thing; concern for the conditions they have to live
in is quite another, and, unlike John Arden, for instance, John Osborne has never tried to dramatize the
predicament of a socially exploited group or to concentrate any of his attention on studying a working-
class background, or in fact any social context. He
focuses so intently on the hero in the foreground that
the group and the background often get blurred.

One of the clearest examples of this is *Epitaph for
George Dillon*, which is the first play I'd like to con-
sider in detail.

PLAYS

Epitaph for George Dillon

 Epitaph for George Dillon, written in collaboration with Anthony Creighton, is a play about a relationship between an artist and an ordinary family. The artist is an actor who's usually out of work. He has something of Jimmy Porter's intensity of analytical self-awareness but none of his courage or his extrovert aggressiveness. Anything but a rebel, he is willing to sell out both as an artist and as a man, and his main ambition is to graft himself comfortably on to a suburban family, first as a sponger and then as a son-in-law. The theme is a promising one and the development of it could have been very interesting if only the two factors in the relationship, George on the one hand and the family on the other, had been seen in the same perspective. But instead, the family is pictured in two-dimensional caricatures of familiar types: the well-meaning mother with her genteel moral principles, the lazy, flirty, brainless teenage daughter with her pop records and her flashy slacks, the unattractive daughter in her middle thirties who has been "let down twice," and the petty, ineffectual father with his *Daily Mirror* philosophy and his mealtime grumbles. The only attempt Osborne makes to create a character who functions on the same level of awareness as George is in Ruth, the aunt. If Josie, the teenage daughter, is the girl George inevitably sleeps with, Ruth is the one he inevitably has his big scenes with. But as a character, she doesn't come off very convincingly either as a member of the family, which she has nothing in common with, or as a Communist who's just left the Party—which is an element in the plot that might well have been scrapped.

All the same, she would have been capable of real give-and-take dialogue with George if only Osborne and Creighton had been interested in writing it. Instead, they make her behave much more like a daydream audience than a real woman.

> Oh, yes, you can be funny, George. These flashes of frenzy, the torrents of ideas, they can be quite funny, even exciting at times. If I don't laugh, it's because I know I shall see fatigue and fear in your eyes sooner or later.

The identification with George is so complete on Ruth's part (and the authors') that we get her speaking exactly the lines that George would have put into her mouth if he had been writing the dialogue.

Consequently, he never properly comes into focus. Is he justified in behaving the way he does? Is society, as epitomized by the family, so incredibly stupid and hidebound that there's nothing the artist can do with it except batten on it? Part of the point seems to be that the actor needs the public more than the public needs the actor, but this is only stated conversationally. Emotionally and dramatically, the family gets scant sympathy compared with George, and even his tuberculosis is dragged in so that it works like special pleading for him at a point in the action when we might have started to dislike him intensely for keeping quiet about being married until after he's got Josie pregnant.

Altogether, Osborne and Creighton are oddly reticent about passing judgment on George. Do they want us to admire him as an artist or condemn him as a parasite? As an actor he is obviously pretty negligible and as a writer all he achieves is a script which succeeds in a low-grade provincial tour after it has been doctored by a grubby theatrical manager.

> BARNEY: To get back to this play of yours. I think it's got possibilities, but it needs rewriting. Acts One and Two won't be so bad, provided you cut out all the highbrow stuff, give it pace—you know: dirty it up a bit, you see.
>
> GEORGE: I see.
>
> BARNEY: Third Act's construction is weak. I could help you there—and I'd do it for quite a small consideration because I think you've got something. You know that's a very good idea—getting the girl in the family way.
>
> GEORGE: You think so?
>
> BARNEY: Never fails. Get someone in the family way in the Third Act—you're half way there.

Yet it may well be that Osborne and Creighton are trying to draw a distinction between George's basic talent and the use he makes of it. Ruth, the most intelligent character in the play, says that he "may be a genius."

And what about George's relationship with Ruth herself? How are we meant to judge his behavior in involving her emotionally and then settling for the pregnant Josie? It seems to be partly in order to prevent this question from arising too forcibly that Ruth is made to move out of the house. If she were on the scene more in Act Three, her physical presence would act more as a criticism of George's conduct, and he would look a good deal less heroic. She's used much more as a foil and as an on-stage audience than as a protagonist. If she stuck to her guns and fought for her right to George's love, he couldn't win anything like as much sympathy as he does in his final scene with her. The writing has a peculiar charm and a pathos which is typical of Osborne and rather anticipates Jimmy Porter.

GEORGE: You know I've been waiting for you to tell me that you're old enough to be my mother. Still, mothers don't walk out on their sons—or do they?

RUTH: How's Josie—have you seen her yet?

GEORGE: God! What a farce! What pure, screaming farce! *(He starts to laugh.)*

RUTH: For heaven's sake!

GEORGE: Sorry. I just thought of something. How to make sure of your Third Act. Never fails! *(Roars with laughter.)* Never fails! *(Subsides almost immediately.)* Don't panic. I'll not get maudlin. I probably would start howling any minute, only I'm afraid of getting the bird from my best audience. *(He looks away from her, and adds in a strangled voice, barely audible.)* Don't leave me on my own! *(But he turns back quickly.)* You haven't mentioned my—success—once.

RUTH: I didn't know whether you expected me to congratulate you or not.

GEORGE: Second week of tour—I've got the returns here. Look: Empire Theatre, Llandrindod Wells —week's gross takings £647 18s. 4d. Long-hair drama gets a haircut from Mr. Barney Evans!

RUTH: I simply can't bear to go on watching you any longer.

GEORGE: But don't you think it's all very comic? I seem to remember some famous comedian saying once that he'd never seen anything funny that wasn't terrible. So don't think I'll mind if you laugh. I expect it. We should be both good

for a titter, anyway. That's why religion is so
damn deadly—it's not even good for a giggle.
And what's life without a good giggle, eh? That's
what I always say! Isn't that what you always
say, Ruth?

RUTH: Let go of my hand. You're hurting me.

GEORGE: Well—isn't it? No. Perhaps it isn't. We
never really had the same sense of humour, after
all.

RUTH: Please don't try to hurt yourself any more
by trying to hit back at me. I know how you feel.
You're overcome with failure. Eternal bloody
failure.

GEORGE: But I'm not a failure, I'm a—success.

RUTH: Are you, George? *(She turns away.)*

GEORGE: Listen! I'll make you laugh yet, before
you go. Just a trip on the stage-cloth, and Lear
teeters on, his crown round his ears, his grubby
tights full of moth-holes. How they all long for
those tights to fall down. What a relief it would
be! Oh, we should all use stronger elastic. And
the less sure we are of our pathetic little divine
rights, the stronger the elastic we should use.
You've seen the whole, shabby, solemn pretence
now. This is where you came in. For God's sake
go. *(She turns to go.)* No, wait. Shall I recite my
epitaph to you? Yes, do recite your epitaph to me.
"Here lies the body of George Dillon, aged thirty-
four—or thereabouts—who thought, who hoped,
he was that mysterious, ridiculous being called
an artist. He never allowed himself one day of
peace. He worshipped the physical things of this
world, and was betrayed by his own body. He
loved also the things of the mind, but his own
brain was a cripple from the waist down. He
achieved nothing he set out to do. He made no
one happy, no one looked up with excitement
when he entered the room. He was always
troubled with wind round his heart, but he loved
no one successfully. He was a bit of a bore, and,
frankly, rather useless. But the germs loved him."
*(He doesn't see Ruth as she goes out and up the
stairs.)*

This is self-dramatizing, self-pitying and sentimental. It depends for its effects on Ruth's being deprived of all critical initiative. Instead of dialogue between them, George is made to take over into his monologues everything that Ruth might have been expected to say and she's made to say in her interpolations everything that he'd want her to say. This is deliberate of course, but the implications are never brought into focus. When Ruth finally walks out on him, this diminishes her stature and leaves him towering heroically, as even a doubtful hero must, over the remaining tiny-minded characters like Josie and Percy and Norah.

The other main fault in the play is the inconsistency of style and structure. Act One begins as if we're in for a family play with the tensions arising out of strains and pressures in personal relationships, and a great deal of material is collected which looks as though it's going to be used later. But it isn't. The themes that are announced in Act One are mostly dropped or rounded off perfunctorily, and the thinning out of plot texture is reflected by the contrast between the beginning and the end. Act One nearly always has quite a number of people on stage at the same time, but Acts Two and Three are given over almost entirely to duets and an occasional trio.

Apart from George, none of the characters is developed in the way that Act One promises. Ruth's affair with the hard-up writer is plotted in quite carefully at the beginning. Although the affair itself is all over before the action begins, we get the device of the watch which her lover has given back and the note that Josie reads, and there's quite a telling scene when Ruth confronts Josie about having taken it. All this starts to get us interested in Ruth for her own sake, but after this she gets very short shrift. She's used in the long duet with George but her own story is continued only very perfunctorily—how she gets herself involved emotionally but not sexually with George and how she decides to leave the family—but it never gets anything like the forefront focus that the build-up prepared for.

With Mrs. Elliot, there's much the same inconsistency. She starts off as an important character. She's the pivot of the household and it's her misplaced maternal instincts which bring George into it. So much is established in Act One about her and her projection on to George of her feelings about her dead son that we expect her to be given a fair amount of space in the foreground so this material can be exploited. But it isn't. Once she's performed her queen-bee function of introducing George into the household, she's as useless as a drone because the play changes its mind about what sort of play it is. Instead of sticking to the same style and the same subject of how George relates himself to the Elliots, it lets itself get seduced partly by George himself, who's given any number of what are virtually solo spots, and partly by characters like Geoffrey Colwyn-Stuart and Barney Evans, who are introduced more or less as interludes. So far as the plot is concerned, Geoffrey never needs so much as a mention and Barney could perfectly well have remained an off-stage character. But since they both have potential for highly entertaining scenes, they're both welcomed right into the foreground. The scenes they dominate are much more like revue sketches in conception than scenes in a three-act play. The main purpose in bringing on Geoffrey is to use him as an opponent for George in an argument about conventional religion, and there's a very good pay-off line at the end when George says he believes in evidence, not faith, and Geoffrey asks him where the evidence is for his talent.

Barney, particularly, is used like a music-hall turn, with George temporarily serving as straight man.

> BARNEY: You take my advice—string along with me. I know this business inside and out. You forget about starving for Art's sake. That won't keep you alive five minutes. You've got to be ruthless. *(Moves into hall.)* Yes, there's no other word for it—absolutely ruthless. *(George follows him.)*
> *(Barney picks up his hat from stand and knocks over the vase. He looks down at the pieces absent-mindedly.)*
> Oh, sorry. Now you take Hitler—the greatest man that ever lived! Don't care what anyone says— you can't get away from it. He had the right idea, you've got to be ruthless, and it's the same in this business. Course he may have gone a bit too far sometimes.
> GEORGE: Think so?
> BARNEY: I do. I do think so, most definitely. Yes, he over-reached himself, no getting away from it. That's where all great men make their mistake —they over-reach themselves.

He's given several very funny lines but the whole approach of the writing has altered radically since Act One. Instead of action and interaction, we have a new, irrelevant character establishing himself through self-displaying monologue.

George's main solo spot comes when he starts to perform on the cocktail cabinet as if it were a cinema organ.

> It looks as though it has come out of a jelly-mould like an American car. What do you suppose you *do* with it? You don't keep drinks in it—that's just a front, concealing its true mystery. What do

you keep in it—old razor blades? I know, I've got it!
(He sits down and "plays" it vigorously, like a cin-
ema organ, humming a "lullaby-lane" style signa-
ture tune. He turns a beaming face to Ruth.)
And now I'm going to finish up with a short selection of popular symphonies, entitled "Evergreens
from the Greats," ending up with Beethoven's
Ninth! And don't forget—if you're enjoying yourself, then all join in. If you can't remember the
words, let alone understand 'em, well, just whistle
the tune. Here we go then!
(Encouraged by Ruth's laughter, he turns back and
crashes away on the cocktail cabinet, pulling out
the stops and singing.)
> "I fell in love with ye-ieuw!
> While we were dancing
> The Beethoven Waltz! . . ."

It's interesting to see how the play breaks up into solo
performances like this because this marks the beginning of Osborne's flight from the restrictive plot
structure of the conventional play into the much
looser techniques of music hall. Especially in his
earlier plays, all Osborne's heroes tend to be per-
formers giving performances. Quite apart from the
vaudeville turns that Jimmy Porter does with Cliff,
all his long monologues are solo performances, with
only a perfunctory interest on Osborne's part in the
reactions of the on-stage audience, and with no question at all of interaction with it. Archie Rice is a
comedian and his off-stage monologues are almost as
full of anecdotes, wisecracks, digressions and reminiscences as his music-hall patter. Luther is also
presented very much as a performer, whose confes-
sions and sermons and deposition at the Diet of
Worms are like solo acts, and who suffers from stage
fright at his first Mass. And the minor characters too
in these two plays—Billy Rice, Phoebe, and Tetzel—
sometimes display themselves in what amount to solo

performances, instead of being established through
dialogue and relationships. But in these two plays,
and to a still greater extent in the later plays, Osborne manages to some extent to discipline the tendency—to make it into a technique. In *Epitaph for
George Dillon* we see it quite literally pulling the play
apart.

Look Back in Anger

Look Back in Anger is the one-man play *par excellence.* Alison, Helena, Cliff, and the Colonel are scarcely allowed any independent life at all. They exist only in relation to Jimmy and they can never have the effect of putting him into any kind of perspective. There's no give-and-take dialogue, hardly any cut-and-thrust dialogue. What we're given is monologue with interruption or monologue with echo.

When Jimmy's in the room, Alison is part stooge and part audience, like Ruth with George. When he's out of the room, she talks of nothing but Jimmy and talks about him in exactly the way that he'd want her to, seeing him as he sees himself.

> I keep looking back, as far as I can remember, and I can't think what it was to feel young, really young. Jimmy said the same thing to me the other day. I pretended not to be listening—because I knew that would hurt him, I suppose. And—of course—he got savage, like tonight. But I knew just what he meant. I suppose it would have been so easy to say "Yes, darling, I know just what you

mean. I know what you're feeling." *(Shrugs.)* It's those easy things that seem to be so impossible with us.

Even in terms of the plot, Alison's behavior follows exactly the lines that Jimmy lays down for it in his aggressive fantasy. At the end of Act One, not knowing that she's pregnant, he says:

> If only something—something would happen to you, and wake you out of your beauty sleep! If you could have a child, and it would die. Let it grow, let a recognizable human face emerge from that little mass of indiarubber and wrinkles. Please—if only I could watch you face that. I wonder if you might even become a recognizable human being yourself.

So, true to the best Trilby form, Alison goes off and has a child and it does die and back she comes to Jimmy.

> I never knew what it was like. I didn't know it could be like that! I was in pain, and all I could think of was you, and what I'd lost. I thought: if only—if only he could see me now, so stupid, and ugly and ridiculous. This is what he's been longing for me to feel. This is what he wants me to splash about in! I'm in the fire, and I'm burning, and all I want is to die! It's cost him his child, and any others I might have had! But what does it matter —this is what he wanted from me! Don't you see! I'm in the mud at last! I'm grovelling! I'm crawling!

Like this, Jimmy finds her quite acceptable.

When she first appears, Helena looks as though she will be able to put up a much better fight than Alison, but, again like Ruth, she allows all her criticism and all the standards she's been upholding to collapse into love the moment she's left alone with him. But once she's been to bed with him—and it's she who seduces him—Osborne isn't at all interested in developing the relationship. There's only one scene before Alison comes back and it's made up of a long section when Jimmy, Cliff, and Helena are all on stage together, a section when Jimmy is alone with Cliff and a very short section (less than two pages of script) when he's alone with Helena. And when Alison comes back, the way Helena's made to behave is more convenient than convincing. She doesn't strike us as a woman who'd simply step aside in favor of Alison's legal claim on Jimmy, and if she did, she certainly wouldn't say:

> Oh, I know I'm throwing the book of rules at you, as you call it, but, believe me, you're never going to be happy without it. I tried throwing it all away these months, but I know now it just doesn't work. When you came in at that door, ill and tired and hurt, it was all over for me. You see—I didn't know about the baby. It was such a shock. It's like a judgement on us.

It's odd that neither of the two relationships with the two women is made anything like so warm or so real as the relationship with Cliff. The negative side of Jimmy's feelings towards Alison is expressed well enough, and so is his initial hostility towards Helena, but the moments of tenderness don't ring true at all with either woman. Quite apart from the embarrassing speeches about bears and squirrels, even the language, usually so straightforward, gets stilted and self-conscious.

> Was I really wrong to believe that there's a—a kind of—burning virility of mind and spirit that looks for something as powerful as itself? The

heaviest, strongest creatures in this world seem to be the loneliest.

But between the two men, everything is more relaxed and natural. When Cliff says "My feet hurt," and Jimmy answers "Try washing your socks," it speaks volumes more about the rough-and-tumble tenderness between them. Cliff has less of a relationship with Jimmy than Alison or Helena has, but what there is of it is much more real.

The only other character in the play is Alison's father, and if anyone was to have been made really hostile to Jimmy, it could most easily have been Colonel Redfern. With his background and his values, he could hardly have had stronger reasons from his own point of view for disliking his son-in-law's behavior. But he's never allowed to come face to face with him, and what he says in Jimmy's absence turns out—disappointingly and not at all convincingly—to be exactly what Jimmy would have wished him to say.

> Perhaps Jimmy is right. Perhaps I am a—what was it? An old plant left over from the Edwardian wilderness. And I can't understand why the sun isn't shining any more. You can see what he means, can't you?

Loose though it is in construction, at least *Look Back in Anger* is fairly consistent in its style. It's obvious, right from the beginning, that this is not going to be a "well-made play" and it's obvious that it's not going to confine itself to what is dramatically relevant. There's going to be a lot of random talk and there's not going to be much dramatic suspense. The action is never going to get going fast enough for us to notice the change of tempo if Jimmy starts reciting lyrics he's written or goes into a Flanagan and Allen or a patter act with Cliff or starts chatting in more or less the manner of a music-hall comedian about the Sunday papers.

> Did you read about the woman who went to the mass meeting of a certain American evangelist at Earls Court? She went forward, to declare herself for love or whatever it is, and, in the rush of converts to get to the front, she broke four ribs and got kicked in the head. She was yelling her head off in agony, but with 50,000 people putting all they'd got into "Onward Christian Soldiers," nobody even knew she was there.

Anything is admissible so long as it's funny enough and not entirely out of character, but the character is much more conditioned by the humor than the humor by the character—which means that any character will always be free to tell any funny story that comes up.

Jokes are very important in Osborne. *The Entertainer*, obviously, is structured around a central character from whom jokes are expected at every throw of the dice and in *Under Plain Cover*, though less successfully, the joke element is again made integral to the organism of the play: the two characters' sexual lives center on acting out a series of jokes. It's not so easy to incorporate jokes into *Luther*: Martin gets slightly out of character when he tells Staupitz about the nobleman who buys an indulgence from Tetzel to cover a sin he hasn't yet committed and who then commits the sin of robbing Tetzel. And in *A Patriot for Me* there are several very funny queer stories worked (aptly enough) into the male ball scene. All in all, the jokes get absorbed into the body of the dialogue fairly easily in *Look Back in Anger* because

the whole play is conceived so very much as a suc-
cession of interludes. The triumph of the play is that
notwithstanding this it makes the smell and atmosphere of the attic flat so real.

As a structure, though, *Look Back in Anger* is an
old-fashioned three-act play with one box set and a
reconciliation in Act Three. There's no departure
from naturalism. The songs aren't alienation effects:
they're embedded in a dramatic context and there's
nothing structural—in fact nothing but the length
of Jimmy's speeches—to interfere with the illusion
that this is life actually being lived out in front of us.

The stagecraft, in fact, is not just conventional, it's
primitive. Instead of making what there is to be
made out of the appearance of a new character, Osborne starts off with three characters already on
stage and lets the other two make their entrances
during act or scene drops. The curtain goes up on
Act Two, Scene One with Helena already installed
in the ménage and on Act Two, Scene Two with the
Colonel already sitting at a table in conversation
with Alison. Nor is there any need for the curtain
to be dropped in the middle of Act Three. Osborne
only uses it to avoid writing the beginning of the
conversation between Helena and Alison. Jimmy
goes out of the room anyway at the end of Act Three,
Scene One, so the scene ends with the two women
looking at each other, and all that happens during
the scene drop is that they've started talking and one
of them has made a pot of tea, which could have been
done during the dialogue, or not done at all. Dramatically it could only be a gain if we saw how they got
from the silence at the end of Scene One to the discussion at the beginning of Scene Two.

Of course these are very small points but they do
indicate how much Osborne was depending on

speeches rather than action to keep the play afloat. Normally one of the most valuable weapons in the playwright's armory is interruption—one character trying to impose his rhythm on another's and perhaps a new rhythm emerging, different from either. But Osborne is chary of letting any of Jimmy's speeches be interrupted except by interjections which help to trigger off the next long monologue.

All the devices for animating the play seem to be built into the engine which gives Jimmy his driving force. As soon as he is off-stage, the play starts to drift, as it does at the beginning of Act Two, when Alison and Helena have a long scene together and Alison gets a lot of long speeches. But her long speeches are completely different in kind from Jimmy's. Instead of displaying her character or her viewpoint, the speeches are used to fill in the past history of her relationship with Jimmy, without letting her speak in a tone of voice which is distinctively her own, the way Jimmy's is his own. Possibly Osborne would have been incapable of characterizing Alison in this way. He makes her tell stories which are unconvincing both in their angling and in their substance about how Jimmy used her to wage a private class war. The description of gatecrashing cocktail parties seems to have been lifted straight out of Philip Toynbee's memoir *Friends Apart* and far too perfunctorily tailored to fit Alison.

> ALISON: They started inviting themselves—through me—to people's houses, friends of Nigel's and mine, friends of Daddy's, oh everyone: the Arksdens, the Tarnatts, the Wains—
> HELENA: Not the Wains?
> ALISON: Just about everyone I'd ever known. Your people must have been among the few we missed out. It was just enemy territory to them, and, as

> I say, they used me as a hostage. We'd set out from headquarters in Poplar, and carry out our raids on the enemy in W.1,S.W.1,S.W.3 and W.8. In my name, we'd gatecrash everywhere—cocktails, week-ends, even a couple of houseparties. I used to hope that one day, somebody would have the guts to slam the door in our faces, but they didn't. They were too well-bred, and probably sorry for me as well. Hugh and Jimmy despised them for it. So we went on plundering them, wolfing their food and drinks, and smoking their cigars like ruffians. Oh, they enjoyed themselves.

The other major weakness in *Look Back in Anger* is that it's not committed in anything like the way that it seems to be. Jimmy Porter makes a huge number of statements on important subjects, political, social, economic, cultural, and religious. But although Osborne obviously thinks of him as basically right-minded, and wants us to do the same, he hasn't written a play which is committed to Jimmy's opinions. The overall movement of the action doesn't throw its weight behind them and it doesn't even show Jimmy as being very deeply committed to them himself. Quite apart from the question of whether there isn't anything more positive he could do than talk about them, the way he settles down at the end into playing bears and squirrels with Alison can only be taken as a retreat into immature emotional coziness. Osborne himself has said that the ending is intended to be ironical, the irony being that this is all Jimmy and Alison have to fall back on, but it doesn't really work in the way he wants it to, and we're left feeling rather let down both by Jimmy and by the play.

The Entertainer

The Entertainer didn't have so much impact as *Look Back in Anger* because there's nothing in it that attacks the audience like the vitriol in Jimmy Porter's monologues. But as a piece of writing for the stage, it's much better constructed and much less conventional. According to Osborne himself, it was the influence of Brecht that first made him dissatisfied with the limitations of naturalism. In any case, he scraps the box set and the whole familiar framework of three-act plotting. The play is still, in fact, divided into three acts, but what's more important is the way that each act is divided into short scenes, which are numbered like acts on a music-hall bill. And in Tony Richardson's production a big figure lit up on either side of the stage to tell us which "number" we were watching. For the first time, the music hall, which Osborne so loves, has provided not just interludes but the spinal column on which the play grows. The action alternates between realistic scenes in the cheap seaside boardinghouse where the Rice family live and much more stylized scenes played by Archie solo at a microphone downstage with a front cloth behind him. He performs as in his comedy spot, with the auditorium and the real-life audience standing in for the music hall and the music-hall audience.

> Don't clap too hard, we're all in a very old building.

Although *Luther* may look the more Brechtian of the two plays, the alienation effects in *The Entertainer* are much apter and work much better in getting us away from the old theatrical "slice of life" illusion. Many of the best moments in Osborne come when he's pulling right away from the conventions of naturalism.

> Let me know where you're working tomorrow night—and I'll come and see YOU.

This is very close to the kind of thing Spike Milligan has been doing in *Son of Oblomov*, confusing and amusing the audiences by involving them directly as he steps in and out of the story frame—except that with Osborne the effect is more under control.

Looking back on *Look Back in Anger* from the vantage point of *The Entertainer*, it's not just the vaudeville sequences but also the monologues that emerge as gestures of protest against the realistic and conventional mold in which the play is cast, and it's only when he's broken this that Osborne is free to refine the technique of exploiting monologue.

In *The Entertainer* there are two distinct kinds of monologue: there are the monologues in the solo scenes and the monologues in the family scenes. In the music-hall solos, as in Bill Maitland's one-sided telephone conversations, Osborne has found a way of dispensing with the on-stage audience. This is always a distraction and an embarrassment. In *Look Back in Anger*, Cliff, Alison, and Helena often have to listen in silence to Jimmy's endless tirades without saying a word and in *Luther* and *Inadmissible Evidence* too, there's a good deal of speechmaking with only the most perfunctory interest on Osborne's part in the reactions of the on-stage listeners.

But in *The Entertainer* the music-hall monologues work very well. There's no difficulty over gear changes, and stories, wisecracks, songs, and political and social comments all fit equally well into the patter, without making Archie sound like a mouthpiece. At the same time, this is Archie's life. Osborne is both saying what he wants to say and showing us his hero in the act of earning his living.

The monologues in the family scenes profit to some extent from our having gotten to know Archie at a different level. There's none of the exasperation we can't help feeling with Cliff and Alison and Helena: Why on earth can't they stand up to Jimmy? But Archie's a professional, and, having seen him in action, we don't so much expect his wife or family to resist his wisecracking domination of them. But of course the monologues inside the family scenes don't work so well as in the solo scenes. The tendency to sermonize is more of an intrusion and in the scene at the beginning of Act Two, for instance, the writing gets noticeably out of character. With a very inadequate springboard (consisting of one line from Frank) Archie is made to dive straight into a big speech about the deadness of the English, which would have been much more in character for Jimmy Porter.

FRANK: You've been away too long. Every night is party night.

ARCHIE: And do you know why? Do you know why? Because we're dead beat and down and outs. We're drunks, maniacs, we're crazy, we're bonkers, the whole flaming bunch of us. Why, we have problems that nobody's ever heard of, we're characters out of something that nobody believes in. We're something that people make jokes about, because we're so remote from the rest of ordinary everyday, human experience. But we're not really funny. We're too boring. Simply because we're not like anybody who ever lived. We don't get on with anything. We don't ever succeed in anything. We're a *nuisance,* we do nothing but make a God almighty fuss about anything we ever do. All the time we're trying to draw someone's attention to our nasty, sordid unlikely little problems. Like that poor, pathetic old thing there. Look at her. What has she got to do with people like you? People of intellect and sophistication. She's very drunk, and just now her muzzy, under-developed, untrained mind is racing because her blood stream is full of alcohol I can't afford to give her, and she's going to force us to listen to all sorts of dreary embarrassing things we've all heard a hundred times before. She's getting old, and she's worried about who's going to keep her when she can't work any longer. She's afraid of ending up in a long box in somebody else's front room in Gateshead, or was it West Hartlepool?

When he says "we" or "people like you," the meaning is meant to spread like ripples from the Rice family to the audience and from the audience to the whole population of England. Osborne's a writer who isn't content to express himself through the particularities of certain characters in a certain situation. He hankers too much after a more direct statement of a more general import. When Archie is talking straight out front he can achieve this, but when Osborne tries to work inside a naturalistic dramatic situation, he is always wanting to break out of it and often destroys it in doing so.

There's the same trouble in the scene where Archie tells Jean about her mother. He describes how she died, and then, with the old Osborne irrelevancy:

> Did I ever tell you the most moving thing that I ever heard?

And off he goes into a story about a Negress blues singer.

> But if ever I saw any hope or strength in the human race, it was in the face of that old fat Negress getting up to sing about Jesus or something like that. She was poor and lonely and oppressed like nobody you've ever known. Or me, for that matter. I never even liked that kind of music, but to see that old black whore singing her heart out to the whole world, you knew somehow in your heart that it didn't matter how much you kick people, the real people, how much you despise them, if they can stand up and make a pure, just natural noise like that, there's nothing wrong with them, only with everybody else.

Olivier came very near to bringing this off—in spite of a word like "oppressed" which belongs to declarations of independence and to political journalism, not to Archie Rice's vocabulary—but finally it's too transparently a statement from the author about the human race, not just a statement from Archie. It's true that Archie has been drinking and it's true that the speech is realistic in having a lot of the sentimental, lapel-pulling vehemence of a drunk who's convinced he has just stumbled on something terribly important about what's wrong with the world. But if

Osborne had intended to relate it only to the situation of the moment, he wouldn't have written it quite like this. He's too intent on riding hobbyhorses to concentrate fully on making Archie real.

He's also too impatient to make journalistic statements about topics he considers important. There's something extremely uncomfortable about all the references to Suez, the Prime Minister who looks like a dog, and the Trafalgar Square rallies. You get the feeling that Osborne might have done better not to aim right at the center of current events but to pick up something from the periphery. And the semi-symbolic resonance that Archie and the shabby music hall have as references to the state of England doesn't fit in at all well with incidents based on news items like the one about the British N.C.O. captured by the Egyptians. There's no question about the genuineness of Osborne's sympathy with the underprivileged people who pay with death or bereavement for the blundering policies of their democratically elected overlords, but the mixture of ingredients is still wrong.

Having to incorporate such arbitrarily chosen materials, the play stands little chance of growing into an organism which can develop a momentum of its own to carry it to a satisfactory end. Act Three is very much below the level of Acts One and Two in quality. Frank's song "Bring back his body and bury it in England" is an utter failure, and Billy's funeral, which follows hard on the heels of Mick's—without any dramatic gain from their proximity—is a very botched piece of stylization. Unwisely, Osborne introduces two new characters into it, Brother Bill and Graham, and we get alternating snatches of two dialogues, Archie's with his brother, and Jean's with her boyfriend. The intention is clear enough but it's too late to launch into a new style, the execution of the scene is clumsy, and the point it's making is unsubtle. It would have been easy enough to make us see Graham as a younger version of Brother Bill (who's too much like Uncle Ben in *Death of a Salesman*) without intercutting between the two dialogues. Both Bill and Graham are presented very glibly and amount to little more than cardboard capitalists. Both are seen as corrupting forces who want to get their victims (Jean and Archie) to go away. Graham wants to marry Jean:

> You're no different from me. You were in love with me, you said so. We enjoyed ourselves together. We could make a good thing of it. I've got quite a decent career lined up. We would have everything we want. Come back with me, Jean.

And Bill wants Archie to go to Canada. Both refuse, as of course they would, and as it's right they should, but it really isn't enough to bring the play to any kind of meaningful conclusion. And the cuts from one dialogue to the other become very awkward.

> ARCHIE: You can never get anything at this Labour Exchange anyway. They must have more bums in this place than in any other town in England. Oh, well, thanks anyway, just two more performances. It's a pity though—I should have liked to notch up twenty-one against the income-tax man. I'll never make my twenty-first now. It would have been fun to get the key of the door, somehow.
>
> JEAN: Here we are, we're alone in the universe, there's no God, it just seems that it all began by something as simple as sunlight striking on a piece of rock. And here we are. We've only got ourselves. Somehow, we've just got to make a go of it. *We've only ourselves.*

> BROTHER: I'm sorry, Archie, but I've given up try-
> ing to understand.
> *(Fade)*

After that, all we get is the final scene in the music
hall.

> There's a bloke at the side here with a hook, you
> know that, don't you? He is, he's standing there. I
> can see him. Must be the income-tax man.

And the faltering reprise of the very good "Why
should I care?" lyric as Phoebe comes on, carrying
Archie's raincoat and hat, to follow him sadly off to
the income-tax man waiting in the wings.

However, even if it does go to pieces at the end,
the structure of *The Entertainer* is a very considerable achievement, and it's a great advance on *Look
Back in Anger* in having minor characters who come
much closer (though still not close enough) to
matching up to the hero in size, interest, reality, and
impact. In fact on this score it's the best of all Osborne's plays to date. Jimmy Porter, Bill Maitland,
Luther, and Redl (in *A Patriot for Me*) are very
seldom off-stage, but in *The Entertainer*, the alter-
nation between the music-hall scenes and the family
scenes encourages Osborne to give time and space to
exploring the other members of the family while
Archie is away at the music hall.

Billy Rice, Archie's father, isn't entirely a character. In substance he's an affectionate elegy on the
vanished graces of the Edwardian era, but this
doesn't stop him from coming to life.

> They were graceful, they had mystery and dig-
> nity. Why when a woman got out of a cab, she
> descended. Descended. And you put your hand out

to her smartly to help her down. Look at them today. Have you ever seen a woman get out of a
car? Well, have you? I have, and I don't want to
see it again, thank you very much. Why I never
saw a woman's legs until I was nineteen. Didn't
know what they looked like. Nineteen. I was
married when I was nineteen, you know. I was only
twenty when Archie's brother was born. Old Bill.
He's got on, anyway. I remember the first time I set
eyes on your grandmother. She was just eighteen.
She had a velvet coat on, black it was, black with
fur round the edge. They were all the fashion just
about then. It was so tight round her figure. And
with her little fur cap on and muff, she looked a
picture.

Like George and Jimmy, Billy is given a great many
set speeches which are long and rhetorical, but for the
first time the rhetoric is characterized and placed.
Osborne is very ambivalent about the period his
grandfather lived in, the twilight of England's imperial greatness and the final heyday of the English
gentleman, but without having quite sorted out his
own feelings, he still manages to put Billy's into perspective, and it's good to find him expending so much
love and care on a character so unlike himself. Osborne sympathizes a lot with Billy's values and he
tellingly invents several situations in which they
come into play as motivations: when Billy tries to
keep Phoebe from talking about Archie's women in
front of Jean, when he intervenes in Archie's relationship with the young girl he wants to desert
Phoebe for, and when he goes back on the stage because Archie needs the money and Billy feels he owes
him something.

Phoebe too has moments of being very moving
and very real, and after the failures of characterization with Ruth and with Redfern, it's impressive that
Osborne succeeds in striking so many notes which

ring absolutely true in her ginny, garrulous, incon-
sequential flow of talk, her rambling reminiscences
of childhood, her drunken touchiness, her differen-
tiation between Jean and her own children—

> I wouldn't take that from Mick or Frank and
> they're my own

her appreciation of Brother Bill—

> It was the way he spoke to me in that quiet
> gentlemanly way and the way he patted my arm

and her fear of never really having anything—

> I don't want to always have to work. I mean you
> want a bit of life before it's all over. It takes all the
> gilt off if you know you've got to go on and on till
> they carry you out in a box. It's all right for him,
> he's all right. He's still got his women. While it
> lasts anyway. But I don't want to end up being laid
> out by some stranger in some rotten stinking little
> street in Gateshead, or West Hartlepool or another
> of those dead-or-alive holes!

It's curious that apart from Mrs. Elliot in *Epitaph
for George Dillon*, Phoebe is the only mother of any
importance in Osborne's work so far, but it is not primarily as a mother that she is seen. She's Frank's
mother and Mick's mother but Mick never appears
and Frank is very unimportant. The mother relationship, which in one form or another is the subject
of practically everything Pinter has written, is something that Osborne has yet to come to grips with in
a play.

In the characterizations of Phoebe and of Billy
Rice, what's unfortunate is that the talent he shows
is not much an ear for dialogue as an ear for mono-

logue. Like Archie, Phoebe and Billy both have their big moments and their big speeches but neither of them really interact with each other or with Archie or with anyone else in the play. Most of the time Archie takes the stage, sometimes Billy and sometimes Phoebe, but none of the rest really get a chance and all we're given is three very good solo lines with descants sung in by other vocalists, never a real duet, never a real ensemble.

Of the other characters, the only one Osborne makes an effort with is Jean. He takes a lot of space to fill in details about the quarrel she's had with her boyfriend in the Trafalgar Square rally and about the art lessons she's been giving in a youth club and about how much she hates royalty, but there's the same inconsistency in the way she's used as there was with Ruth. In Act Two she's only a catalyst-cum-confessor in the big duet with Archie, and in Act Three, in spite of introducing her boyfriend into the action, Osborne takes no real interest in the development of her story. The part couldn't have had three better or three more different interpreters than Dorothy Tutin, Joan Plowright, and Geraldine Mac-Ewan but none of them was able to bring Jean to life as an individual.

All the same, though, I think the achievement of *The Entertainer* has been underestimated, as compared with that of *Look Back in Anger*, which has been overestimated. In Jimmy Porter, Osborne created a voice that got through to thousands of people, but as a character, Archie Rice is the more impressive creation, although once again the most distinctive thing about him is the tone and flavor that the writing gives to his voice. Even in repertory productions, without Olivier in the part, and even in a German translation I saw in Berlin, with Martin

Held playing the lead, there was something in Archie's voice that no one but Osborne could have put there.

> JEAN: You're not serious! You couldn't do that to Phoebe—not a divorce.
> ARCHIE: Children! (*Laughs.*) Children! They're like the bloody music hall. Don't worry about your old man—he's still a bit worried about young Mick. At least, I suppose he is. I told you, nothing really touches me. As the man said, I've paid me one and saxpence—I defy yez to entertain me! Let anyone get up there and give a performance, let them get up, I don't care how good it is. Old Archie, dead behind the eyes, is sitting on his hands, he lost his responses on the way. You wouldn't think I was sexy to look at me, would you? Well, I 'ave a go, lady. I 'ave a go, don't I? I do. I 'ave a go. That barmaid in the Cambridge. That barmaid who upset poor old Billy in the Cambridge—I had her! When he wasn't looking . . .

This is full of sentiment and self-pity, but they're partly justified by the fact that Archie is drunk. The manner of speaking is every bit as rhetorical, self-conscious and self-dramatizing as George Dillon's or Jimmy Porter's but under the pathos and vulgarity, the pain is much more genuine. The deadness and the desperation establish a tone of voice which is new in our theater.

The World of Paul Slickey

It wasn't at all surprising that after introducing so many lyrics and song-and-dance routines into *Look Back in Anger* and *The Entertainer* Osborne should turn next to a musical. The surprise was that *The World of Paul Slickey* should be such a flop. The management chose Bournemouth, of all places, to open the pre-London tour and there the audience was puzzled but polite. They obviously felt that the rock-and-roll funeral was in bad taste and they didn't know how to take all the business about changes of sex, but there was nothing to compare with the wars waged across the footlights once the show got to the West End. There was shouting and booing and, one night, an actress gave a two-finger sign to the audience. People in the balcony got very annoyed when a lot of the upstage action and dancing turned out to be invisible to them, except for the actors' feet, and the duet "We're going to screw the Income Tax Man" seems to have been crucial in the escalation of general hostilities. But what first got the whole audience into an irritable state was sheer confusion.

The most confusing thing about *The World of*

Paul Slickey is that it's split down the middle, almost like an Elizabethan play, into two separate plots. One is about Mortlake Hall and the evasion of death duties; the other is about journalists and their invasion of privacy. The one tenuous connection between the two is that the gossip columnist Jack Oakham (Paul Slickey) figures in both. He's married to Lord Mortlake's daughter, so his boss, who knows he's "got connections" with the family, sends him to see what's going on. He thinks that perhaps the old man, who gave his entire estate to the family, may be dead but that they may be trying to keep quiet about it for another forty-eight hours so that a full five years will have elapsed since the transfer of the property. The action shifts between Mortlake Hall, where Jack is having an affair with his wife's sister, and the newspaper office, where he's having an affair with his secretary, but the fact of having one hero who is common to both halves of the play does very little to offset the discontinuity. Elizabethan audiences were used to subplots, but modern audiences aren't, and Osborne hasn't given them anything like the help they need to keep up with his complicated story.

To add to the confusion, he often has his characters talking or singing about subjects that have nothing at all to do with what's happening on the stage at that particular moment, and he hardly ever allows himself time to establish one theme, even verbally, before rushing on to the next. The first scene in Mortlake Hall is an example. It opens with Jack and Deirdre in bed together. But they hardly have any dialogue about themselves before they're talking (satirically) about Deirdre's husband, Michael, and Jack's wife, Lesley, and how brave Lady Mortlake is. As we haven't yet met any of these three characters, none of the satire can work very effectively, and some of the jokes sink to a very low level.

JACK: You didn't wake up Michael when you left?

DEIRDRE: Good lord no. Nothing wakes Michael. He just lies in bed all night, mumbling his beastly political speeches in his sleep. Oh, it's awful, I can't tell you!

JACK: Poor darling.

DEIRDRE: Do you know what he actually said to me the other night? He suddenly grabbed my shoulder in the middle of the night, and said "away with party labels and let us pull together." Oh, darling what are we going to do?

JACK (*looking at sheets*): Make the bed I suppose. We've lain on our bed—and now we must make it.

DEIRDRE: Oh, Jack for heaven's sake—!

JACK: Sorry, darling.

DEIRDRE: It's just that these last few weeks have been so horrid what with having to be polite and casual with Lesley when she was here. I think she suspects.

JACK: I don't believe it.

DEIRDRE: What do you know about her! You're married to her.

JACK: I've known her like a rabbit knows an eagle.

DEIRDRE (*stands*): I think you're a little hard on her, darling. After all, she may be your wife, but she's my sister. I dare say she's been a little upset about daddy. Just like we all have.

JACK: He's all right now, isn't he?

DEIRDRE: The doctor says the crisis has passed, but one still can't be quite sure when he'll collapse again. Why, the slightest thing might—

JACK: I didn't realize you were all so fond of him.

DEIRDRE: Of course we're fond of him—and Mummy's been so terribly brave.

JACK: Yes, she's always been a brave soul.

DEIRDRE: She has. I remember how she was when they gave away India. But she's been even more wonderful this time. Why, sometimes she seems

so serene. I've wondered if she's been aware of
what is going on around her.

The whole structure suffers from the same indis-
cipline. Osborne is like a butterfly hunter who loses
interest in each specimen the moment he has it in his
net, hardly caring if it escapes as he rushes off in
pursuit of the next. The elastic plot is stretched to
embrace an impossible variety of characters he dis-
approves of: a Conservative Member of Parliment
(Nigel in the flesh), a randy old peer, his wife who
does nothing but arrange flowers and coming-out
parties, a blackmailing priest with a passion for eating, an ex-trade-unionist butler, a pop singer, and a
glamorous brassiere manufacturer. With a mass of
targets like this in his line of fire, any writer would
find it hard to pick them all off, but not satisfied with
what he's already got, Osborne impatiently levels
his sights at another whole host of random topics:
Godfrey Winn, British heroism as portrayed in war
films about the navy, capital punishment, the illegitimate children of British monarchs, changes of
sex, and stage censorship. He couldn't bear to leave
out anything he could satirize, especially anything
which could be lumped, however loosely, under the
heading conservatism. Mrs. Giltedge-Whyte, an ex-
mistress of Lord Mortlake, turns up to demand "a
fair deal" for herself and the daughter he has fa-
thered with her. But within two minutes of her first
entrance, she's sidetracked into a long lyric about
capital punishment and well within the first minute
of their conversation together, Lord Mortlake is
made to say:

Why, only a few weeks ago I started an influ-
ential movement to step up the stage censorship.

The trouble is that with all these splenetic salvos of righteous indignation discharged so energetically all over the battlefield, the socialite gossip columnist who is intended to be the main target escapes with just a few slight satirical scratches. In fact he actually gets protected by Osborne. With so many subjects to handle, there's no time or space to dramatize the case against Jack, so it has to be stated verbally, mainly by Jack himself. This has the effect of glamorizing him with inner conflicts and guilt feelings, which we're implicitly asked to respect. Osborne is by now so hooked on the hero habit that Jack Oakham emerges as a frustrated idealist.

> There must be something I can do,
> Something to believe,
> Something better, something matters,
> There's someone to grieve,
> Somewhere better, somewhere finer,
> There must be something I can do!

The lyrics in general are disfigured by the same headlong impatience to get from one subject to the next without stopping to think whether the composer and the audience would be able to stand the pace. The lyrics are very different from the ones in *Look Back in Anger* and *The Entertainer*, which consist much less of didactic statements, much more of expressions of mood, coupled with a humorous tendency on the characters' parts to make fun of themselves.

> I'm tired of being hetero
> Rather ride on the metero
> Just pass me the booze.
> This perpetual whoring
> Gets quite dull and boring
> So avoid that old python coil
> And pass me the celibate oil.

Or:

> Why should I care?
> Why should I let it touch me!
> Why shouldn't I, sit down and try
> To let it pass over me?
> Why should they stare,
> Why should I let it get me?

But the lyrics in *Slickey* are all too liable to fall in love with their own arguments. As one statement leads to the next, the song often gets pulled out to inordinate length, right away from the mood and context. One or two of the lyrics are very good, like "Beautiful Things" and Jack's lyric about "living from mouth to mouth," with the refrain

> Tell me later,
> Don't tell me now.

But Michael's "It's a consideration we'd do well to bear in mind," which is based on the good idea of making him sing entirely in clichés, gets far too involved, protracted and wordy:

It's a consideration we'd do well to bear in mind
We can safely say in a not unpompous way, blind
Them with words! When there are things you can't mention,
Say "The Government is giving this matter its most grave and urgent attention"
If they're concerned about the atom
Simply hurl some clichés at 'em
If a problem's in a pressing condition
Give them words by the ton and the year—give them a Royal Commission.

And this, unfortunately, is typical.

The failure of *The World of Paul Slickey* lies in the self-indulgence and the haphazard mixture of ingredients. Osborne describes the show as "a Comedy of Manners with Music," but the observation of contemporary manners is very superficial indeed,

with each type represented by a cliché and no genuine interest in taking a fresh look at the social scene.
Osborne's material is concocted out of the script of an
earlier, unproduced play, an indignity he suffered
personally at the hands of journalists, and a host of
random prejudices, jokes and ideas. Most of the
prejudices are familiar, some of the jokes are funny
while some are very cheap, and several of the ideas
are brilliant. But the occasional flashes of brilliance
are poor compensation for the messy organization.
The only sequences in the show which unequivocally
worked as a whole were some exciting dance routines, especially in "The Mechanics of Success." For
the rest, it was a matter of good lines and good moments swallowed up in an irritating chaos of in-
discipline.

A Subject of Scandal and Concern

Osborne's television play, *A Subject of Scandal and Concern*, was broadcast by the BBC in November 1960, eighteen months after the failure of *The World of Paul Slickey*. It tells the story of George Holyoake, a young teacher and lecturer, who was the last man in England to be imprisoned for blasphemy. The play takes up his story just before he made the remarks that led to the prosecution—in answer to a question at the end of a lecture—and it ends with his release from prison.

In some ways the play serves as a sketch for *Luther*. In outlook, George Holyoake was about as far removed from Martin Luther as anyone could be, and of no comparable importance, but to Osborne both men had something of the same appeal in that they both fought single-handedly against the conformist pressure put on them by both their friends and their enemies, and in both of them the heroism is highlighted by a physical disability. In Holyoake's case, it's a bad stammer, but, like Bill Maitland in the nightmare sequence at the beginning of *Inadmis-*

sible Evidence, he insists on conducting his own defense at his trial.

The story is pieced together out of short scenes, which are linked by a narrator, who is made to speak very patronizingly to the television audience.

> Good evening. I am a lawyer. My name is unimportant as I am not directly involved in what you are about to see. What I am introducing for you is an entertainment. There is no reason why you should not go on with what you are doing. What you are about to see is a straightforward account of an obscure event in the history of your—well my—country. I shall simply fill in with incidental but necessary information, like one of your own television chairmen in fact. You will not really be troubled with anything unfamiliar. I hope you have been reassured.

And this is how he sums the action up at the end:

> This is a time when people demand from entertainments what they call a "solution." They expect to have their little solution rattling away down there in the centre of the play like a motto in a Christmas cracker.
> (*He starts folding up a manuscript, and puts it into a briefcase.*)
> For those who seek information, it has been put before you. If it is meaning you are looking for, then you must start collecting for yourself. And what would you say is the moral then?
> (*He picks up the case and starts to go.*)
> If you are waiting for the commercial, it is probably this: you cannot live by bread alone. You must have jam—even if it is mixed with another man's blood.
> (*The door opens and a policeman's feet appear.*)
> That's all. You may retire now. And if a mini-car is your particular mini-dream, then dream it. When your turn comes you will be called.

Good night.
(*He walks out. The camera follows him and pans up to a close-up of the policeman standing at the door. The Narrator walks deliberately down the prison corridor to his client.*)

The reference to commercials is a hangover from the original intention of showing the play on commercial television, and the final shot of the Narrator walking down the prison corridor is something else that wasn't adjusted to fit the final production, in which John Freeman played the part in modern clothes, more or less as a "television chairman."

The construction of the play shows a lot of signs of haste and carelessness, particularly in the first of the three acts, where the short scenes follow each other like episodes in a cartoon-strip history. We see Holyoake and his wife at her sister's house in Cheltenham, where they're staying, and although they're paying for their keep, their sick child isn't being given enough to eat. We see Holyoake giving his lecture to a local branch of the Social Missionary Society on "Home Colonization as a means of superseding Poor Laws and Emigration." And then we get the Narrator reading from the report on the meeting in *The Cheltenham Chronicle.*

A teetotaller named Maitland got up and said the lecturer had been talking a good deal about our duty to man but he omitted to mention any duty towards God, and he would be glad to know if there were any chapels in the community. The Socialist then replied that he professed no religion at all and thought that they were too poor to have any. He did not believe that there was such a Being as God and impiously remarked that if there was, he would have the Deity served the same as the Government treated subalterns, by placing Him upon half pay.

Next in the patchwork assembly of scenes comes one with the brother-in-law, who's introduced into the action just for the sake of having him read a paragraph from the next number of *The Cheltenham Chronicle* to the effect that the local magistrates regard it as a clear case of blasphemy and have decided to prosecute. Then we have another short scene in which the police superintendent enters another hall where Holyoake has been winding up a meeting. Twelve men take up their positions at the back of the hall. We get a scene with Holyoake in the dock of the magistrates' court, a scene in the jail, where the head of police lets a local surgeon question him on his opinions, and one in the county jail, where two magistrates come to try to persuade him to compromise.

> COOPER: Think on it, Holyoake. The judge will put you down and not hear you.
> JONES (*kindly*): Come, boy. You are a deist, are you not? (*Pause.*) You cannot be something else. Can you?
> HOLYOAKE: I don't know, sir. I did not know before and I do not know now. But I do think that I am alone in this matter and will remain so.

The whole of Act Two is taken up by the trial, so the Narrator is only heard commenting, never seen, because there is no linkage needed. The play builds up plenty of evidence of prejudice against Holyoake in the jurors, the witnesses, and the judge, whose summing-up barely stops short of telling the jury how to decide. Holyoake has a long rhetorical speech in which the style of the writing comes very close to that of *Luther*.

> This blasphemy then is an antiquated accusation. What a turmoil, what a splutter there was in this

land when men first said they would not eat fish,
that they would not bow down to priests, and that
they would not confess except when they liked.
What threats there were of Hell and flames, what
splashing about of fire and brimstone, what judge-
ment on these men choked with their beef steak on
a Friday. Such frying, such barbecueing and everyone dripping in a flood of sin and gravy and not the
smallest notion of a red herring anyway. How
fathomless must be the patience of Heaven that this
island is not swallowed up in the sea for it, when
we know we shall appear in the next world with so
much mutton on our heads! But we have tried to
look into the rules with the intelligence that has
been given to us and calculated the risk that eating
mutton can no longer be a blasphemy. If God be
truth you libel Him and His power! It is a melan-
choly maxim in these courts of law that the greater
the truth the greater the libel, and so it would be
with me this day if I could demonstrate to you that
there is no Deity. The more correct I am, the
severer would be my punishment because the law
regards the belief in a God to be the foundation of
obedience among men.

The act ends with the sentence being passed—six
months.

At the beginning of Act Three, there is an effective scene where we see Holyoake in the common
room of the jail being very furtive about scratching
himself. He's caught the itch from his fellow pris-
oners and he knows that if they find out, the cure
will be to be dipped naked into a barrel of brimstone and pitch. "After this," the Narrator tells us,
"the prisoner was left to lie for days in blankets already used by a hundred others smeared in the same
way." We get the inevitable scene with the chaplain,
when Holyoake refuses to pray, a scene with Jones,
who brings the news that Holyoake's daughter is
dying, and a scene with his wife, which stresses the

point that Holyoake is absolutely on his own. She blames him for the child's death and has no sympathy at all for the predicament that his integrity has got him into.

> When you leave this place you will walk over the grave of your own child. Well? Where is your tongue now, Mr. Holyoake?

As a documentary reconstruction of a little-known incident of nineteenth-century history, the play is quite interesting, but it doesn't amount to anything more than that. Richard Burton's understanding and very gentle performance as Holyoake added a great deal to Osborne's characterization, making a lot of useful capital out of the stammer and engaging sympathy without pathos. But the script subordinates the development of the hero's personality to the rather predictable plot. As soon as we've had our first few glimpses of the forces and prejudices lined up against Holyoake in each quarter, we know what the outcome will be. It is one that could have been the basis of a far better play in the hands of a playwright concerned to ask why these forces were lined up against Holyoake and to analyze the answer in social terms. But the background stays badly out of focus. The treatment of the foreground is clear but scrappy, and the total result is a play no better than many television plays and a narrator even more tiresome than most television narrators.

Luther

Luther is just as much a one-man play as *Look Back in Anger*, with the difference that the one man doesn't emerge as clearly. In some places, the writing of the central part rises to energetic bursts of vivid identification with Luther, but it's still left very much to the leading actor to make him emerge as a rounded personality. Part of the trouble is that the writing doesn't give him an individual voice. In everything that Jimmy Porter or Archie Rice or Bill Maitland says, the tone is unmistakable.

> Mummy and Daddy turn pale, and face the east every time they remember she's married to me.

> Well, as I was saying, before my ignorant old Father interrupted—

> And as for necking, I never went in for it, never would, and pray God I am never so old, servile or fumbling that I ever have to wriggle through that dingy assault course.

Even with short excerpts like these, no one who knows the plays would have any difficulty in identifying the speakers. Sometimes, of course, they sound very much like each other, especially on the subject of sex. Bill and Archie, particularly, are fond of talking in much the same way to anybody who happens to be listening about how much and how often they like it. Which helps them to emerge as flesh and blood, even if it's the same flesh and blood. But with historical characters, like Holyoake and Luther, Osborne doesn't have the basic confidence in his writing of the part to let a speech pattern emerge naturally. The only distinctive characteristic of Holyoake's way of speaking is his stammer, and this disappears in his big speech to the court in Act Two. Otherwise, his language varies, as Luther's does, between passages of quotation, which sound like what they are, and passages of Osborne, which sound very modern.

Like the language, the whole characterization consists of jigsaw pieces which don't fit together. Osborne leans heavily on a psychoanalytical interpretation, *Young Man Luther* by Erik H. Erikson, which was published in England in 1959, and it is from this that he derives his emphasis on psychophysiological factors, explaining Luther's revolution against the Church in terms of a persistent identity crisis in which the constipation, the epilepsy, and the conflict with the father are all interrelated.* The dependence on Erikson explains why the parts of the play dealing with Luther's private conflicts are so

---

* In a very valuable article called "Luther and Mr. Osborne" in the *Cambridge Quarterly* (Volume One, Number One), Gordon Rupp points out that there is no evidence at all of epileptic attacks, which seem to be a fabrication of hostile Catholic biographers, and that there is no evidence of constipation until after Luther left the monastery. Erikson accepts the epilepsy stories because they fit his theory of the "epileptoid paroxysm of the ego-less."

much better than the parts dealing with public conflicts. He is convincing as an individual rebel, but
not as a leader capable of getting half of Germany
on his side. When Staupitz sums up Luther's achievement at the end of the play we feel incredulous and
bewildered.

> The world's changed. For one thing, you've made
> a thing called Germany; you've unlaced a language
> and taught it to the Germans, and the rest of the
> world will just have to get used to the sound of it.
> As we once made the body of Christ from bread,
> you've made the body of Europe, and whatever our
> pains turn out to be, they'll attack the rest of the
> world too. You've taken Christ away from the low
> mumblings and soft voices and jewelled gowns and
> the tiaras and put Him back where He belongs. In
> each man's soul. We owe so much to you.

The play as a whole hasn't contained anything to
substantiate this dramatically, and Osborne's Luther
hasn't established himself as a personality capable
of doing what the historical Luther did.

The best act is the first and this is the one which
is intended as an investigation of the internal and
unconcious conflicts. Osborne never quite succeeds in
getting a clear focus on the relation between Luther's rejection of his father and his rejection of the
Church, but the long argument with the father
which is the climax of the act gives a good pointer to
Luther's memories of the boy's frustrated love for
the man.

> You disappointed me too, and not just a few
> times, but at some time of every day I ever remem-
> ber hearing or seeing you, but, as you say, maybe
> that was also no different from any other boy. But I
> loved you the best. It was always *you* I wanted. I
> wanted your love more than anyone's, and if any-

one was to hold me, I wanted it to be you. Funnily enough, my mother disappointed me the most, and I loved her less, much less. She made a gap which no one else could have filled, but all she could do was make it bigger, bigger and more unbearable.

We see how this could lead to a projection of the same combination of emotions towards God: a sense of desperate need and a sense of being singled out for special victimization. Whether the punishment comes from God or from the Devil is immaterial.

MARTIN: Somewhere, in the body of a child, Satan foresaw in me what I'm suffering now. That's why he prepares open pits for me, and all kinds of tricks to bring me down, so that I keep wondering if I'm the only man living who's baited, and surrounded by dreams, and afraid to move.

BRO. WEINAND (*really angry by now*): You're a fool. You're really a fool. God isn't angry with you. It's you who are angry with Him.

The growing isolation of Luther in the monastery is shown very well. The intensity of the internal pressure leads to an exorbitant guilt for which confession is an inadequate safety valve. A man like this would not get much help from his brother monks personally or from communal religious practices or from submission to the authority of his superiors. All authority is irksome to him and there was never any chance of his sinking his feelings of being special into a sense of membership in a group. In that negative aspect, Luther does stand out as an individual, but the isolation becomes much more real than any kind of positive commitment, even to God. Luther's relationship with God is rather like Jimmy Porter's with Alison: what's made very real is the resentment, the feeling of giving everything and getting nothing back except hatred or indifference, but the moments where Osborne tries to build up a positive feeling of love don't work at all.

> Oh, God! Oh, God! Oh, thou my God, my God, help me against the reason and wisdom of the world. You must—there's only you—to do it. Breathe into me, like a lion into the mouth of a stillborn cub. This cause is not mine but yours. For myself, I've no business to be dealing with the great lords of this world. I want to be still, in peace, and alone. Breathe into me, Jesus. I rely on no man, only on you. My God, my God do you hear me? Are you dead? Are you dead? No, you can't die, you can only hide yourself, can't you? Lord, I'm afraid. I am a child, the lost body of a child. I am stillborn. Breathe into me, in the name of Thy Son, Jesus Christ, who shall be my protector and defender, yes, my mighty fortress, breathe into me. Give me life, oh Lord. Give me life.

This phrase "the lost body of a child" runs through the play like a motif.

> I lost the body of a child, a child's body, the eyes of a child; and at the first sound of my own childish voice. I lost the body of a child; and I was afraid, and I went back to find it. But I'm still afraid. I'm afraid, and there's an end of it! But *I* mean . . . (*shouts*) . . . Continually!

What Osborne's Luther feels more than anything is a nostalgia for childhood, with its combination of innocence and dependent love for a strong protecting father. It is because he never experienced this love himself that he hankers after it so much and he expresses his fantasy of what it would be like in the description of Abraham and Isaac in the sermon at the end of the scene with the Knight.

> Abraham was—he was an old man . . . a . . .
> very old man indeed, in fact, he was a hundred
> years old, when what was surely, what must have
> been a miracle happened, to a man of his years—a
> son was born to him. A son. Isaac he called him.
> And he loved Isaac. Well, he loved him with such
> intensity, one can only diminish it by description.
> But to Abraham his little son was a miraculous
> thing, a small, incessant . . . animal . . . aston-
> ishment. And in the child he sought the father.

And this of course prefigures the final scene of the
play when Luther is talking to his own infant son.

> You should have seen me at Worms. I was al-
> most like you that day, as if I'd learned to play
> again, to play, to play out in the world, like a
> naked child. "I have come to set a man against his
> father," I said, and they listened to me. Just like a
> child. Sh! We must go to bed, mustn't we? A little
> while, and you *shall* see me. Christ said that, my
> son. I hope that'll be the way of it again. I hope so.
> Let's just hope so, eh? Eh? Let's just hope so.

But even here, in this intensely private scene, Osborne finds it necessary to drag in a reference to
Worms, and this is typical of the whole play. The
main themes are all worked out in personal terms
but, after the end of Act One, the angling, the selection of incidents, the treatment, the structure, and
the style are all dictated by his determination to concentrate on the historical issues, which don't really
interest him.

Compared with Brecht's *Galileo* or John Whiting's
The Devils, for instance, Osborne's *Luther* isn't a
historical play at all. In their different ways, Brecht
and Whiting both devote a great deal of time and
energy and love to re-creating a solid historical actu-
ality, and whether the details are accurate or not,

the stage is effectively steeped in period atmosphere
and filled with a wide-angle view of people doing
business, practicing their religion, eating, suffering,
doubting, fighting. Osborne misses out completely
on the social element. And whereas Galileo and
Grandier are both presented as products of their
period—rebels against it, certainly, but still conditioned by it in the way they think and feel—Osborne
starts with what he sees as a neurosis and then perfunctorily sketches in a period background. Tony
Richardson tried hard to reinstate the sixteenth century in the production but, encouraged perhaps by references to Holbein and Dürer in the stage directions,
he presented it in a very static visual way, much more
in terms of groupings and backdrops than of life or
movement. He gave us plenty of vivid scenic detail—
the animals in the hunting scene and the rich robes
at the Diet of Worms—but history remained obsti-
nately on the backcloth. It would be interesting to see
a production of the play by Joan Littlewood or Planchon or any other antiheroic director who works
mainly in terms of the group. But no director could
alter the fact that the conflict in the foreground is a
solo fight between one modern man and his anx-
ieties. Luther emerges as a rebel against everything,
including history.

Not that Osborne is alone in using historical subjects in this way. Around 1960 several English dramatists were writing period plays in which heroism was
largely equated with isolation and the isolation was
absolute: one man versus the time he is living in. The
hero is a man of uncompromising integrity who can
find nothing to connect with in a corrupt and compro-
mising society. Either he gives up and withdraws from
political and public life or else he refuses to give up
and gets martyred, like Bolt's Sir Thomas More in

A Man for All Seasons, Whiting's Grandier in *The Devils*, and for that matter, Rattigan's Ross. Osborne's Luther follows very closely the pattern set by Brecht's Galileo. Galileo recants, while Luther defies the Pope, but he compromises over the Peasants' Rebellion and both plays end with a scene showing the ex-hero passive in the comfort of a private home with a well-meaning woman there to distract him from his bad conscience with good food.

Whether he finally compromises or not, this kind of hero obviously appealed to an audience which identified with Jimmy Porter's feeling that there was no cause left good enough to die for. This is the basic difference in attitude between the protest plays being written in the late 1950's and the left-wing plays of the thirties which committed themselves to helping history along faster. For them, the main pressures affecting motivations were social and economic, so the stress was not on the individual personality. For Osborne, personality stands right in the foreground and the main determining factors are physiological and psychological. The hero's natural condition is isolation and his natural form of expression is monologue, so it follows that historical context, social context, economic context, and even the context of surrounding personal relationships are reduced to the level of incidentals which may be used in the development of the hero's personality or as functions of the storytelling, but they will not be factors in his development.

It's extremely odd that Brecht should have come into fashion among English playwrights just at the time when they were getting involved with this approach to history. Of course, it was not *Luther* that started the vogue for Brecht. Kenneth Tynan and Joan Littlewood had done a lot to introduce his ideas into England, and Osborne's reaction against naturalism in *The Entertainer* (1957) was one of the results of their canvassing for Brecht's cause. Then, in 1960, *A Man for All Seasons* started its long run, and in the preface to the published edition Robert Bolt explicitly acknowledged the influence:

> The style I eventually used was a bastardized version of the one most recently associated with Bertolt Brecht.

The next year Osborne went one further and came out with a play that many people saw as the most Brechtian that had ever been written in the English language. *Luther* consists of twelve self-contained scenes, and in Tony Richardson's production, each one was introduced by a Knight who came on stage with a banner to announce the time and place of the action. In his selection of scenes, Osborne attempted a Brechtian sweep and span, choosing a wide variety of settings to show his hero in contrasted circumstances, starting with him as a novice and ending shamelessly close to the final scene in *Galileo*.

But basically, with its ideas, themes, and even most of the key quotations* taken from a book by a

---

* Gordon Rupp has pointed this out. Erikson writes:

And so, as Martin put it, the praising ended and the blasphemy began.

Act One, Scene Two ends with the sounds of Mass beginning off-stage as Luther comes back with a naked child in his arms and advances towards the audience to say:

And so, the praising ended—and the blasphemy began.

Erikson quotes a line from one of Luther's sermons:

He gorges us with great eagerness and wrath. . . . he is an avaricious, gluttonous fire

which Osborne uses in the scene with Weinand:

He's like a glutton, the way he gorges me, he's a glutton. He gorges me, and then spits me out in lumps.

LUTHER | 67

psychoanalyst, *Luther* isn't Brechtian at all, despite
the similarities of structure and surface. Osborne
makes exactly the same mistake as Bolt made in
thinking that a series of borrowed Brechtian tricks of
styling and staging could be made to fit a completely
different kind of play, which isolates the hero's personality from its social and historical context.

Brecht's technique was worked out for his so-
called Epic Theater, which is a form that could have
been evolved only by a Marxist. It belongs very
much to the time it was created, the late twenties
and thirties—a point which has been ignored by
many of the more adverse critics of Brecht. Brecht's
theater is utterly different from the contemporary
English theater in its interests and intentions. With
its historical approach and its preoccupation with
social and economic issues, the only insights it gives
us into individual behavior are in terms of the extent to which it's conditioned by external pressures,
political and societal. Individuality is at a low
premium in this market and the whole repertoire
of alienation effects was built up to prevent audiences
from identifying with the characters. If Mother
Courage stops in the middle of her sufferings to sing
a song, this is partly to remind us that we're watching an actress playing a part on a stage, and the
interruption of the illusion is essential to Brecht's
purposes, which are to make the audience think

And Osborne even puts a quotation from Nietzsche which he
finds in Erikson into Luther's mouth.

As Nietzsche put it "Luther wanted to speak to God directly,
speak as himself and without embarrassment."

This becomes:

When I entered the monastery I wanted to speak to God directly, you see. Without any embarrassment, I wanted to
speak to him directly.

rather than feel. But if the Common Man talks directly to the audience and changes his costumes on stage or if Tetzel hawks his indulgences to the stalls or the Knight recites the stage directions, the device may be an effective theatrical flourish but it is not intended to interfere with the belief or the sympathy that the heroes command. Unlike Brecht, Bolt and Osborne are both identifying completely with their heroes and want audiences to do the same.

Of course, Brecht wasn't the originator of Epic Theater or of the chronicle method. Shakespeare used it. His histories are written in short scenes which span a vast range of time and different locations as they tell the stories of the heroes' careers. Considering *Luther* simply as a piece of storytelling, it's a very bad failure, lacking even the clarity of *A Subject of Scandal and Concern*. The monastery sequences are easy to follow but the story line gets very muddled afterward, especially in Act Three. We're never told how Luther came to leave the monastery or where or how he then lived. The whole of Act Two and the first scene in Act Three are taken up with the battle over indulgences. In itself, this is sketched very clearly, step by step. We see Tetzel in action; there's a scene where Staupitz plants the fact that Luther has been preaching sermons about indulgences and urges him to go gently; we then see him preaching a sermon and ignoring the warning; there is the scene in Augsburg where he is summoned before Cajetan, who tries with great charm and skill to make him bow to the Pope's authority; we meet the Pope himself at a hunting lodge, where he dictates an order for Luther to be excommunicated unless he can either be made to submit or brought into custody in Rome; we see him burning the papal bull and preaching a defiant sermon; and

finally, in the scene at the Diet of Worms, Johan von
Eck debates with him in the presence of the Emperor Charles V and Luther refuses to retract unless
they can expose his errors in the light of the Scrip-
tures. These scenes make it look as though the whole
Reformation arose out of a defiance of papal authority that hinged simply on the issue of indulgences.
There is one passage at the end of a sermon about
indulgences which describes how Martin was sitting
on the lavatory one day thinking about a text and
fantasying about a rat slashing at his privates, when
the inspiration came to him, "The just shall live by
faith." (After which his bowels functioned.) Gordon
Rupp has calculated that there are ten references to
sweating, four to vomiting, fourteen to the movement of Luther's bowels, and five to justification by
faith.

After the Diet of Worms scene, the narrative goes
completely to pieces. With a leap of four years to
1525, one dead peasant on a cart, an anachronistic
marching hymn, and some off-stage cannon shots
and shouting, we have nothing except a long monologue from the Knight to tell us what happened, and
it's extremely difficult either to understand what the
Knight is meant to stand for or to make sense of his
monologue, even if you already know something
about the Peasants' Rebellion. He is talking to the
dead peasant.

> Anyway, it never worked out. Did it, my friend?
> Not the way we expected anyway, certainly not the
> way *you* expected, but who'd have ever thought we
> might end up on different sides, him on one and us
> on the other. That when the war came between you
> and them, he'd be there beating the drums for *them*
> outside the slaughter house, and beating it louder
> and better than anyone, hollering for *your* blood,

cutting you up in your thousands, and hanging you up to drip away into the fire for good. Oh well, I suppose all those various groups were out for their different things, or the same thing really, all out for what we could get, and more than any of us had the right to expect. They were all the same, all those big princes and archbishops, the cut rate nobility and rich layabouts, honourable this and thats scrabbling like boars round a swill bucket for every penny those poor peasants never had. All those great abbots with their dewlaps dropped and hanging on their necks like goose's eggs, and then those left-over knights, like me for instance, I suppose, left-over men, impoverished, who'd seen better days and were scared and'd stick at nothing to try and make sure they couldn't get any worse. Yes . . . Not one of them could read the words WAY OUT when it was written up for them, marked out clearly and unmistakably in the pain of too many men. Yes. They say, you know, that the profit motive—and I'm sure you know all about that one—they say that the profit motive was born with the invention of double entry book-keeping in the monasteries. Book-keeping! In the monasteries, and ages before any of us had ever got round to burning them down. But, you know, for men with such a motive, there is only really one entry. The profit is theirs, the loss is someone else's, and usually they don't even bother to write it up.

The colloquial language and the twentieth-century speech patterns don't make it any easier to understand what he's talking about. No audience could possibly guess from this scene why or how the peasants rebelled or in what sense Luther let them down. This familiar charge against him is taken over from Erikson, and altogether Osborne seems to have done hardly any reading outside the one book.

This is not important in itself, except as indicating how limited his interest in the subject must have been. He was in love, as always, with the idea of defiance of authority, and the main attraction of Luther as a subject must have been his success in flouting the authority of the Establishment—one man who divided the world into two camps. But Osborne's Luther is a man whose motivations have very little to do with exterior reality. The characters in the play who are meant to stand for the various authorities against which Luther rebelled are mere papier-mâché figures. Except of course the working-class father, who is the only one of the other characters in the play who is developed into anything more than a feed or a foil or a one-scene cameo. Weinand and Staupitz are both like good television interviewers: they ask the right questions to cue in the best possible display of personality and they show the right sympathy. Tetzel certainly makes an impact, but only in his monologue and only in a revue-sketch kind of way. The subtlest writing comes in the scene with Cajetan, but this is made up more of interlocking monologues than of dialogue, while many of Cajetan's speeches are explanations of Luther to Luther, an extra interpretative gloss on his personality, thinly disguised as a scene between two characters. The Pope and von Eck are typical Osborne caricatures, and Katherine, Luther's wife, is extremely shadowy.

The play was treated with enormous respect by most of the critics.

Plays for England

The short two-act play *The Blood of the Bambergs* and the one-act play *Under Plain Cover* were produced together at the Royal Court under the title *Plays for England*. They represent two more experiments in different styles. Unfortunately, Osborne is more interested in trying the styles on than in wearing them, and even in short pieces like these, he never keeps the same one on for the whole length of the play.

The Blood of the Bambergs is a satire on royalty in socialized England. It pokes fun at some of the national extravagances: the extravagance of having a monarchy at all and then having to divert building labor away from schools and houses when preparations have to be made for occasions like state funerals and royal weddings. But Osborne found he couldn't make all the points he wanted to make inside the main body of the action, so he put in a long preamble of commentary in which a television reporter called Wimple, modeled on the late Richard Dimbleby, describes the scene in the cathedral on the eve of a royal wedding and then puts questions to the foreman in charge of the workmen and to the newly appointed Minister of Culture. In themselves these scenes are well done in a revue-sketch kind of way, especially the opening parody of Dimbleby rhetoric.

> They have been labouring into the night in prep-
> aration for the tremendous events of the morrow.
> For what they are doing is, indeed, a labour of
> great love, as great as that which impelled those
> men seven centuries ago when they applied their
> ancient skills and crafts to the building of this
> great cathedral for the remembrance of man and to
> the glory of God. For in a few hours' time—twelve
> and a half to be exact—and on this very spot, the
> moment which millions of people throughout the
> world have awaited with such expectation will ar-
> rive and two very famous people will be united in
> holy matrimony; and united amid all the pomp
> and splendour that a proud and grateful nation can
> provide on such occasions for her most illustrious
> ones.

But it all takes far too long. We are over halfway through the first act before the story begins to get going with the news that the Prince, the bridegroom of tomorrow, has killed himself in a fast car.

The way the plot then develops is more typical of Whitehall farce than of Whitehall politics. It's de-cided that the wedding must nevertheless take place and the reasons given are that the Prince's only brother is too homosexual to provide any heirs and that the publication of the truth might bring down the government. So a replacement groom has to be found very quickly. Fortunately, there is a bearded Australian photographer who has been sleeping peacefully in the cathedral all through the television interviews and all through the desperately worried conference that the Minister of Culture has with Colonel Taft, the Guardian of the King's Household

—who appear to have the affairs of state entirely in their hands. And fortunately, the bearded Australian photographer turns out to be an illegitimate son of the late King, with such a striking resemblance to the dead Prince that all they have to do is shave him.

It's a daring and very funny idea, which produces a few very funny scenes. The scene in the palace where the Australian, who keeps tripping over his sword, is being persuaded by Colonel Taft to go ahead with the impersonation is like a good music-hall sketch.

> RUSSELL: A good question. I can't remember my lines, and I can't stop this bloody sword swinging between my legs.
> TAFT: Where's your manhood?
> RUSSELL: Doing all right till this morning, thank you, mate.

And Princess Melanie is given some devastating lines, which were beautifully spoken at the Royal Court by Vivian Pickles in a hilarious imitation of the Queen's voice.

> My whole weary system is spinning around forever like a royal satellite in a space of infinite and enduring boredom. Oh, my God, I am so bored! (*She goes to the window.*) I am so bored, do you hear me, my people? My countrymen, I am so bored, and most of all, I am bored with you, my people, my loyal subjects, I am so bored that even this cheap little Australian looks like relieving it for a few brief moments, now and then, in the rest of my lifetime.

But there's not enough high comedy to sustain the play's two acts and the different styles of vaudeville, satire, parody, and farce don't really blend either with each other or with the bizarre scene in which an Ordinary Woman (housewife and mother of three) emerges from a laundry chute in the palace, so full of adoration for the Prince that she threatens to shoot herself unless he'll sleep with her—and does so when he refuses. Graham Crowden, as the Colonel, was splendidly unperturbed by the dead body, but a play cannot survive on three or four splendid moments and as a whole it never came together. The idea was better than the execution of it.

Under Plain Cover suffers from much the same inconsistency and, being a one-act play, shows it up all the more glaringly. More than any other Osborne play, it gives the impression of being written too fast—as if he'd started writing without more than a rough idea of what he was going to do and continued without giving himself enough time to go back and revise.

The first fifteen minutes of the play are a Genet-inspired exercise in the dramatic exploitation of shared fantasy. It's rather diluted by comparison with Genet and terribly lacking in Genet's drive to penetrate to the ultimate depths of any situation he takes up, but it has its amusing moments. We're shown a young couple, Tim and Jenny, who get their fun out of dressing up in different costumes and acting out scenes accordingly—a doctor and his maid, a boxer and a girl guide, a motorcyclist in a black leather jacket, and a pregnant bride. But after letting them act out the first situation, the doctor and the maid, Osborne drops the idea, and the conversation between them changes to a protracted series of jokes about knickers, in which it couldn't matter less who says which lines. Some of the jokes are clever, some are bad, some are puns, some are parodies of newspaper advertisements, and sometimes the effect is very much one of padding—for instance when they start speculating about what kind of underwear the Lady Almoner would have worn at the hospital where Jenny had her last baby. The best part is the parody of the BBC critics in a discussion on underwear, even if the idea derives from N. F. Simpson's parody of The Critics in *A Resounding Tinkle* and from Peter Sellers's long-playing record. In any case, the substance derives from actual reviews of Osborne's own plays.

> TIM: It seems to me that these knickers are speaking out of a private, obsessional world—full of meaning for them. But has it any significance for us? I think not. On the whole, a dull, rather distasteful evening.
>
> JENNY: Not without quality. On the other hand, I would not say straight out it had no quality at all. What do the others think?
>
> TIM: Doesn't seem to have found an entirely satisfactory form for what they are trying to say. The reason for the elastic is never clearly or adequately explained.
>
> JENNY: By no means a total artistic success.
>
> TIM: I thought them schoolgirlish and sniggering. Very tiresome indeed. At least bikinis are brief! It's all very vigorous in an undisciplined way. One does get so tired of these chips on the gusset. Very self-indulgent and over-strident, especially in the length of leg, I thought. Colour was reasonable, but surely Herbert Farjeon did these with much more taste and economy?
>
> And after all, this frenetic destructiveness is hardly helpful. What do they really offer to put up as an alternative? We are left unsatisfied with questions posed and nothing answered.
>
> Hear, hear! This sour soufflé certainly failed to rise for me. Although everyone tried hard enough. I suppose what they were aiming at was pure lingerie. Ah—you mean like pure cinema. Exactly, and then, of course, there's the obvious influence of Genet. Indeed. To say nothing of:

James
Ionesco
Fanny Burney.

Troise
—and his mandoliers* too. Let's not forget
them. That influence is quite clear.

In itself this is very good, quite as good as anything
you're likely to get in a good undergraduate revue,
but the standard of the wit is no higher than that
and so far as the play is concerned it doesn't get us
any further. It's a case of two characters being used
to put over a good joke; it doesn't carry on with
what the opening of the play started—two people
living a joke.

After this, the play falls completely to pieces.
There's a stylized birth of a baby behind a screen,
exactly as in Ann Jellicoe's *The Sport of My Mad
Mother*, and then we get a complete change of style
and subject. As if fantasies and fetishism weren't
enough to be getting along with, Osborne brings in
incest and newspapers. A choric newspaperman, who
made a brief appearance earlier on to cover a gap
while Tim and Jenny were changing costumes, an-
nounces to the audience that though they don't yet
know it themselves, Tim and Jenny are actually
brother and sister. At this point Osborne loses all
interest in them and rides off on his hobbyhorse
about the destructiveness of the Press's intervention in
private lives. After showing us so much about Tim
and Jenny from inside, he never again gives us so
much as a glimpse into their consciousnesses. They
are both quite literally reduced to the level of figures
in a tableau, puppets manipulated by the exploiting
power of the Press, which is personified by the down-

* "Troise and His Mandoliers" was the name of a well-known
British band.

at-heel reporter Stanley, who takes over the whole
play. The substance now consists of a narrative by
him, illustrated with devices like banners lowered
from the flies and Jenny speaking like a newspaper
article she's supposed to have written herself.

> STANLEY: Well, I phoned the office and I said I can
> give you the exclusive story of the girl who
> married her brother, signed by her. I think you'll
> want to use it on page one.
>> Drop banner with Headline—
>> I MARRIED MY BROTHER
> They did.
> JENNY: I am the girl who married her brother.
> Yes, the handsome man who is the father of my
> two darling baby boys is my father's child, my
> mother's son.

In contrast to the leisurely scenes of their life together which opened the play, the reporter's narrative now disposes of nine years in the space of a few
minutes, telling the audience how Jenny married
another man, with the newspaper paying for the
wedding reception—tableau of a wedding group
being doused with rice, photographed, etc.—and how
she finally came together with Tim again. They live
together secretly in a little suburban house in Leices-
ter until the newspaper catches up with their secret,
and the play leaves them with the reporter once
again on their doorstep.

JIMMY, Kenneth Haigh, and CLIFF, Alan Bates, play the fool as ALISON, Mary Ure, tends to the ironing in the 1956 London production of *Look Back in Anger*.

Scene from English Stage Company production of *The Entertainer* with Brenda de Banzie as PHOEBE, Laurence Olivier as ARCHIE, and Joan Plowright as JEAN.
SUNDAY DISPATCH

The 1958 New York production of *Epitaph for George Dillon* starred Eileen Herlie as RUTH GRAY and Robert Stephens as GEORGE DILLON, a role he created in London.
ZODIAC

Albert Finney as MARTIN in the London production of *Luther*. Two years later, in 1963, he triumphantly repeated the role in the New York production.
SANDRA LOUSADA

The Blood of the Bambergs, one of two *Plays for England*, 1962, starred Vivian Pickles in the role of MEL-ANIE and John Meillon as RUSSELL.

Maximilian Schell, standing, center, as ALFRED REDL, attends a transvestite ball in a scene from the New York production of *A Patriot for Me*.
MARTHA SWOPE

Opposite: Scene from the London production of *Inadmissible Evidence* with Nicol Williamson as MAITLAND and Cyril Raymond as HUDSON, a role created by Arthur Lowe.
DOMINIC

Among those spending a long weekend in *The Hotel in Amsterdam*, Royal Court Theatre, 1968, are Paul Scofield as LAURIE and Judy Parfitt as ANNIE.
DOMINIC

A Patriot for Me

The triumph of *A Patriot for Me*, compared with *Plays for England*—and compared with any other Osborne play—is that it achieves much more integration. It's a conventional piece of construction. If *Luther* adopts the manner of Brecht's epic style, *A Patriot for Me* goes back to Goethe's—with its sequence of short scenes to advance the story by showing the hero in different sets of circumstances. But stylistically there's more consistency than usual. And what's completely new, for Osborne, is that we see the central character more through other people's eyes than his own. It's still a one-man play. Redl monopolizes just as much of the action as Jimmy Porter or Archie Rice or Luther or Bill Maitland, but he doesn't commandeer it the way they do and he's not used as a mouthpiece for Osborne's opinions and attitudes. He doesn't even talk much about his feelings. Shyer and less extrovert than the other heroes, he goes out of his way to adapt himself to the situation he's in and the people he's with. Most of the time he's saying less than half of what he feels and all through Act One he's less than half aware of what he feels.

This presentation of him is a piece of very shrewd restraint on Osborne's part. With his enormous talent for encouraging an audience's sympathy towards a hero and with the strong sympathy he obviously feels himself for the homosexual, it must have been very tempting to create a much more heroic hero and this would have made it easy to condone his weaknesses by blaming them on social and professional pressures put on him as a sexual non-conformist. But he makes no attempt to do this. Redl is presented without comment or apology as he works his way up the military ladder to the rank of colonel, and as he becomes a traitor. The Russians pressure him into working for them by threatening to expose his homosexuality, which would ruin his military career. When he's confronted with the choice, we don't see him making up his mind, but we don't need to. It's quite consistent with what we already know about him that he would opt for treachery and face both the decision and its consequences with panache.

Yet for all Redl's weaknesses, Osborne makes him very likable in the script—much more likable than Maximilian Schell made him in his stiff performance at the Royal Court. He is endowed with all the qualities that make for popularity, so when we're told how much the other officers like him, we believe it on the strength of what we've seen for ourselves. He cuts a dashing figure, attractive, impulsive, cynical, charming, urbane, capable of warmth and humor, brave enough to risk acting as second for an officer who is known to be Jewish, but careerist enough to put on a good show of anti-Semitism when promotion is at stake. That Redl is Jewish himself is something we only learn from the program note: the play is not concerned to make the point.

The way that Redl's homosexuality is planted is

very clever indeed. Throughout the whole of the long first act, we see nothing of it except that his relationships with women tend to be infrequent and unsatisfactory. In the scene at Madam Anna's, it seems to be more shyness than anything else that keeps him talking to the waiter instead of hurrying upstairs to the pretty girl Taussig has lined up for him and when he's finally making love to her, it doesn't go well. He nearly faints, and leaves in the middle of the night. In the affair with Countess Delyanoff, we know that something is wrong. She's genuinely passionate about Redl—though her detailed reports to the Russians provide a nice ironic counterpoint to her ardor—but he's unable to reciprocate. He drinks heavily and refuses to make love with the light on and gets nightmares and moans out in the middle of the night. But still we don't know what it is that's wrong.* Then there's the scene in the café, where Redl refuses the chance Taussig offers him of a girl at the opera and gets accosted by a young man —"I know what you're looking for." But there's nothing conclusive until the end of the act, when we find him in bed with a young private soldier.

The trouble is that once this revelation has been made, the technique changes slightly. Act One consists entirely of short scenes, ten of them, but three quarters of Act Two is taken up by one long scene which, for all its brilliant shock effects and for all its virtuosity in importing a Danny la Rue gaiety into *fin de siècle* Viennese transvestitism, remains quite

* Or at least we wouldn't if it weren't for the appalling side effects of reviews and pre-publicity which, with this as with so many plays, effectively prevent the dramatist from giving us the information he wants us to have in the order he wants us to have it. Our reaction to Redl is substantially different because we already know that *A Patriot for Me* is a play about homosexuality. But that is not Osborne's fault.

unfunctional in taking the play or the portrait of
Redl any further. There is quite a lot of fairly static
conversation about homosexuality and the second
scene in Act Two is devoted to a rather feeble parody
of Freud lecturing on homosexuality. The third and
final scene in Act Two is the confrontation in which
the chief of Russian espionage forces Redl to choose
between becoming a traitor or a civilian. But the
whole work of building up to this is done almost entirely by Act One, and scarcely at all by Act Two.

Once he has made his decision, it's fairly predictable that the play will end with discovery and
death. But Act Three gives us neither the tension of
inner uncertainty that we had when he hadn't yet
discovered himself nor the suspense of external
events moving dramatically towards his destruction.
What the play as a whole lacks is a vantage point
from which Osborne can snipe at both internal insights and external incidents. He seems to have gone
too far towards abandoning a technique which depends on explicit self-revelation without yet having
acquired enough skill in developing a plot from outside. The individual moments in Act Three which are
most effective are moments when Osborne reverts to
the monologue technique (which he didn't use at all
in Act One or Act Two) and identifies completely
with Redl's viewpoint. And it comes as a surprise
when he does this because we're not used to emotional outbursts or self-exposure from Redl—

Well, I didn't love you. I love Stefan. *We* just
fooled one another. Oh, I tried to hoax myself too,
but not really often. So: tonight's your wedding
night. (*Pause.*) I tell you this: you'll never know
that body like I know it. The lines beneath his
eyes. Do you know how many there are, do you
know one has less than the other? And the scar be-

hind his ear, and the hairs in his nostrils, which has the most, what colour they are in what light? The mole on where? Where, Sophia? I know the place here, between the eyes, the dark patches like slate—like blue when he's tired, really tired, the place for a blow or a kiss or a bullet. You'll never know like I know, you can't. The backs of his knees, the pattern on the soles of his feet. Which trouble him, and so I used to wash them and bathe them for hours. His thick waist, and how long are his thighs, compared to his calves, you've not looked at him, you never will.

Nor is it done just in this one scene where at least there is the justification that the Countess is pregnant by an ex-boyfriend of Redl's who is now going to marry her. It happens again in the scene with Viktor, which consists almost entirely of the outburst, and it's just thrown at us without any previous build-up in the plot.

You're so stupid you thought you could catch me with a shoddy ruse like that. You'll get no bills paid, nor your automobile, that's the bottom of it, you're so avaricious, you'll get nothing. You're so worthless you can't even recognize the shred of petty virtues in others, some of which I have still. Which is why you have nothing but contempt for anyone, like me, like me, who admires you, or loves you, or wants and misses you and has to beg for you at least one day a fortnight. Yesterday, yesterday, I spent two excruciating hours at the most boring party at Mohl's I've ever been to, talking to endless people, couldn't see or hear, hoping you— God knows where you were—that you'd possibly, if I was lucky, might turn up. Just hoping you might look in, so I could light your cigarette, and watch you talking and even touch your hand briefly out of sight.

It's impossible not to admire Osborne's courage in

writing speeches like this when so many playwrights
have taken cowardly cover in working out a homosexual theme in terms of a heterosexual variation.
But he still hasn't found the right way of blending
the private and the public elements, the self-revealing monologues and the external incidents. The worst
breakdown of the storytelling is the puzzling scene in
the hospital with Mischa Lipschutz. We have had a
perfunctory build-up to this in a conversation with
Kupfer but nothing nearly enough to justify the
presence of the scene, which seems to have been put
in for the sake of some very self-indulgent writing of
mad dialogue. It may be, as Mary McCarthy suggested in her review of the English production in
The Observer, that Osborne wanted to show that
homosexuality "can lead to madness" but this seems
a vague and unlikely point for him to make.

> MISCHA: I've been here quite a long time. I don't
> quite know how long, because we're absorbed
> into the air at night, and then, of course, they
> can do anything they like with you at will. But
> that's why I keep rather quiet.
> REDL: Who, Mischa?
> MISCHA: They do it with rays, I believe, and atoms
> and they can send them from anywhere, right
> across the world, and fill you up with them and
> germs and all sorts of things.
> REDL: Mischa, do you know where you are?
> MISCHA: On a star sir, on a star. Just like you. I
> expect you were sent to Vienna too, sir, because
> you are the same kind of element as me. The
> same dual body functioning.

As for the minor characters, there's not much interest in developing them. The one who comes off
best is the Baron, who throws the party in Act Two.
His way of speaking is dangerously close to that of

the contemporary middle-aged London homosexual but the language just manages not to clash too violently with our image of Viennese aristocracy half a century ago, and George Devine's performance gave a splendid lift to the play. The writing of the Countess's part gives her more facets and more dignity than most women in Osborne, but Jill Bennett was a strange choice for the part. The senior officers in the Austrian army are quite effective cameos, if sometimes a little reminiscent of Staupitz and the wish-fulfilment way he acts as a substitute father to Luther. The Russian Colonel comes off very well, too, and George Murcell's performance stood out with George Devine's above the general level of the acting.

The production as a whole rather let the play down. The awkwardness of the scene changes was underlined by the awkward and inconsistent use of a gypsy band to bridge some of them, and generally very little atmosphere was evoked, except in the ball scene. Worst of all, though, was the failure to bring out any of the undercurrents in the writing. Each scene was directed very much at its face value and this heightened the impression of discontinuity, especially in Act Three. This is particularly unfortunate because the overall intention of the play is rather unclear in the writing, so it badly needed a director who could push it into a sharper definition. As it was, different people came away from the Royal Court with wildly different ideas of what it was that Osborne was trying to say.

In the other plays, even in *Luther*, the statement that the play is making always emerges clearly, sometimes too clearly and often too soon—if his last acts are invariably a letdown, part of the reason is that everything has already been said—but what is the real purpose behind *A Patriot for Me?* He obviously wanted to make some sort of statement about patriotism and treachery together with some sort of statement about homosexuality and heterosexuality. But as we see from the ball scene, practically everyone in the play is homosexual, soldiers and civilians, senior officers and subalterns, solicitors and waiters, so there's no danger of the audience's making any facile equation of homosexuality with a lack of loyalty. The only inference we can make from the title is that Osborne wants us to see Redl as the truest kind of patriot—the man who's willing to betray his country out of loyalty to his real self, but this idea isn't really integrated into the play.

According to Kenneth Tynan:*

> Osborne's intention was to show the pressures exerted on sexual deviants by social prejudice; . . . he was not blaming the queer but the society that outlaws queerness.

If this is true, the play fails for the same reasons as *A Subject of Scandal and Concern*: Osborne is blaming society without taking the trouble to look at it. The minor characters add up to a very inadequate representation of the social background, and with the protagonists consisting almost entirely of homosexuals, there's no one but Oblensky and Dr. Schoepfer to stand for the heterosexual male. Oblensky is sexually gross and an outsider to Austrian society, while Schoepfer's place in the play is very puzzling indeed. Quite apart from the question of any *volte-face* on Osborne's part—making a Freudian into such a caricature after relying so heavily on an exorbitantly Freudian interpretation in *Luther*—it's understand-

* In a letter to *The Observer* (July 18, 1965) replying to Mary McCarthy's review of the play.

able why in this context he should want to ridicule the Freudian attitude to homosexuality. But why does the play end with a scene in which we see Oblensky taking the same kind of interest in Schoepfer as he had earlier in Redl? Nobody's been able to explain this satisfactorily and Tynan's interpretation is ingenious but evasive.

> The implication here is not, as Miss McCarthy wildly suggests, that Freud was "a homosexual or a Russian agent"; it is that the Freudian approach to sexual deviation (as a disorder to be cured by analysis) is not only pointless but reactionary, since it transfers the responsibility for homosexual unhappiness from society to individual upbringing, thereby confirming society in its belief that queers have only themselves to blame.
>
> Hence (Osborne hints) the continued public support for laws that permit men like Vassal to be blackmailed for their proclivities.

These are very good points but they aren't points that the play succeeds in making. If it's true, as Tynan says, that the play repudiates "loyalty to Freud and loyalty to country (the twin bastions of Western civilization)," the repudiations are not very forceful because they are not very coherent. Except for the Schoepfer scenes and the Mischa Lipschutz scene, the story line itself is very clear—and in this sense the play is an advance on *Luther*—but it doesn't take the meanings that Osborne, and Tynan, try to hang on to it.

Inadmissible Evidence

In some ways *Inadmissible Evidence* is better than anything else Osborne has written, but the mixture of styles and conventions is very messy. It starts off with a confusing, unrealistic nightmare sequence which is far too long in itself and which has very little connection, stylistically or thematically, with the play that follows. It shows that Bill is anxious and guilty, afraid that the Law Society is after him and, at some level, wanting to be taken to task. He couldn't bear it if there were no one capable of sitting in judgment on him. But the scene comes nowhere near to being justified by the little that the subsequent story gains from it.

The rest of the play zigzags between naturalism and stylization, without ever managing—or even particularly trying—to establish a convention by which the shifts could be made into an asset. Immediately after the nightmare sequence, there's a long sequence which is completely naturalistic, establishing the routine of life in the office. Then suddenly, just over halfway through the play, we find that the action on the stage is now being pictured through the

distorting lens of Bill's vision. He's becoming incapable of focusing clearly on external reality and
the device of having three different divorce clients
played by the same actress forces us inside his muddled mind. But the three scenes with the three women
are played on different levels of stylization. The first
one, Mrs. Garnsey, is interviewed more or less re-
alistically, but we see that Bill can't concentrate on
what she's saying without being paralyzingly re-
minded of himself.

> MRS. GARNSEY: You see, he's a good man really. He's
> kind, he's very sensitive indeed, he seems to be
> one step ahead of me all the time in everything,
> everything. He always has been. He loves me. I
> know that . . . I think we . . . Well, I . . . dis-
> appoint him. But no more than he disappoints
> himself . . . He *is* clever, he does his job well. He
> works hard. He's good looking. He has a lot of
> charm, in his own way, he really has, he can
> make you laugh like almost no one else. But
> what, what kills me is that he is being hurt so
> much.
>
> BILL: How do you mean?
>
> MRS. GARNSEY: By everyone. He comes home to me,
> and I know that nothing really works for him.
> Not at the office, not his friends, not even his
> girls. I wish they would. God knows, he tries
> hard enough. I wish I could help him. But I
> can't, and everyone, everyone, wherever we go
> together, whether it's a night out, or an evening
> at our club, or an outing with the children, every-
> one's, I know, everyone's drawing away from
> him. And the more people have been good and
> kind and thoughtful to me, the worse it's been
> for him. I know. And now. Now: *I'm* doing the
> same thing. The children hardly notice him. And
> now it's *me*. I can't bear to see him rejected and
> laughed at and scorned behind his back and ig-
> nored— (*All this last is scarcely audible.*) And
> now it's *me*. I've got to leave him.

In the scene with the second client, Mrs. Tonks, we get a stylized interweaving of quotations from the divorce petition (read by the woman) and from a reply of her husband's (read by Bill), so that each point is answered as it's made and each answer seems to be applying both to Mr. Tonks and to Bill himself.

> MRS. TONKS: That the respondent refused to cease from having intercourse during the time of the petitioner's menstrual periods at 42 Macwilliam Street and number 11 Wicker Street, notwithstanding the petitioner's entreaties . . .
>
> BILL: There were difficulties between us. Such that my wife failed to reach satisfaction.
>
> MRS. TONKS: That. On frequent occasions at the said addresses whilst he was having intercourse with petitioner he did . . .
>
> BILL: My wife visited the Marriage Guidance Council on at least three occasions who told her they believed the difficulty was due to my wife's reluctance . . .
>
> MRS. TONKS: Notwithstanding the fact that he knew the petitioner found this conduct revolting and upsetting.
>
> BILL: We've none of us been reluctant much have we? Well, there were girls like Maureen, and even with you there were difficulties but not revolting or upsetting. At least, not much, I don't think so. You weren't reluctant, you should be happy, you didn't cling on to it like it was the crown jewels. You were generous, loving, bright, you should have been able to cope. *I* should have been able to cope.
>
> MRS. TONKS: He told the petitioner he liked to hear the noise made by . . .
>
> BILL: To have another child. Another child. In spite of the advice given her by the Council she refused to use this.
>
> MRS. TONKS: That. It was his desire to have sexual intercourse with a woman in this street to whom he referred . . .
>
> BILL: Because she said it was nasty. Nasty and messy.

And then with the third client, Mrs. Anderson, we get completely unrealistic dialogue as if it had just that minute occurred to Osborne that he could develop the technique he used for the quotations still further. The result is like two people taking turns at a game of free association.

> MRS. ANDERSON: Things became increasingly unhappy and difficult when my husband gave up his job and became a traveller for a firm in electrical fittings. He was able to be at home most of the time, but when he was away, never more than for the odd day or two, he would accuse me of going out with men.
>
> BILL: Well. She thinks I've got mistresses all over London. They both do. And it's not even true. Worst luck. No, thank God.
>
> MRS. ANDERSON: He said I ought to go out on the streets.
>
> BILL: You might have met me then. You might have been worse off.
>
> MRS. ANDERSON: I have never been with anyone apart from my husband.
>
> BILL: That's what's wrong with all of you, you dim deluded little loving things. You listen to promiscuous lady journalists and bishops and your mother. And hang on to it.
>
> MRS. ANDERSON: But he's always saying these things.
>
> BILL: He listens.

At the end of the conversation we see Bill dismissing the three women much more as if he were chasing ideas out of his brain than clients out of his office. But the graduated stylization of the three scenes is not so easy to take because we become aware of it as a literary device.

Then, after the three women, a male client, Maples, gets Osborne back on to his homosexual hobbyhorse and the play is allowed to change direction completely. The technique goes right back to the method of characterization of *The Entertainer*. Maples, like Billy Rice and Phoebe, is developed through long, self-revealing monologues. It's dangerously easy to fall into writing like this in a lawyer's-office setting, where the lawyer can ask questions, as Bill does here, reducing himself for the purposes of this one scene to the level of a typical Osborne minor character. This wouldn't matter so much if the scene were relevant, but it doesn't give us any new light on Bill, who is made to sympathize, as Osborne does, with the young man for not being able to live out his own sexual life without interference from the police. And we are made to see Maples on a different level of reality from the three women that we've seen through the distorting lenses of Bill's vision. Maples we see as he sees himself. And whereas it's useful to the play to make the same actress play all three divorce clients, it was anything but helpful to double Maples with Jones, the young solicitor. John Hurt at Wyndham's did a very much better job on both parts than the original actor at the Royal Court, but Nicol Williamson's incredulous stare when he entered as Maples came close to unintended comedy.

The scene with the daughter, which follows, is stylized in yet a new way, with the unfortunate young actress having to move about the stage and react and be hugged and toss her head and finally go, without ever uttering a syllable. This is a convention which is only sustained for the one scene, so it's hardly a convention at all, but it neither fits with the realistic parts of the play nor with the stylized scenes with the divorced clients. It succumbs fully to two common Osborne temptations: using the hero as a mouthpiece for all sorts of opinions which don't particularly belong to him and dragging on a new character just as a representative of a type. Jane may start off as Bill's daughter but she's very soon standing in for the whole of the younger generation.

> You are unself-conscious, which I am not. You are without guilt, which I am not. Quite rightly. Of course, you are stuffed full of paltry relief for emergent countries, and marches and boycotts and rallies, you, you kink your innocent way along tirelessly to all that poetry and endless jazz and folk worship, *and* looking gay and touching and stylish all at the same time. But there isn't much loving in any of your kindnesses, Jane, not much kindness, not even cruelty, really, in any of you, not much craving for the harm of others, perhaps just a very easy, controlled sharp, I mean "sharp" pleasure in discomfiture. You're flip and offhand and if you are the unfeeling things you appear to be, no one can really accuse you of being cruel in the proper sense.

The scene also provides the perfect example of how much less dramatic his monologues are when they are addressed to an on-stage character. Anna, Bill's wife, never appears at all, but from the way he talks to her over the telephone, she becomes much more real than Alison does in *Look Back in Anger*, while the appearance of Liz at the end of the play actually destroys much of what has been built up by Bill's telephone conversations with her. It's a badly written scene, jolting us back into naturalism again, and it makes impossible demands on the actress, who has to embody the love that Bill needs but can't accept. It takes us right back into the George Dillon world of wish-fulfilment dressed up in flesh and blood as a woman.

If Osborne ever had any reason for thinking that he could integrate all these *ad hoc* stylizations into one dramatic organism, it must have been based on the intention of breaking the naturalistic progression of the story down as the hero breaks down, asking us to see everything disintegrating, including the play, through the disintegrating vision of Bill. There's a stage direction in the printed script which says that in some of the long telephone conversations, the audience should sometimes be in doubt about whether or not there is anyone at the other end of the line. Anthony Page's production didn't quite bring off this effect, but Nicol Williamson's performance certainly gave us the growing hysteria of losing touch with reality and the writing went on forcing us to identify with Bill's unsteady consciousness in a way that was often most effective theatrically. But the method breaks down when, besides showing us everything through Bill's subjectivity, Osborne asks us to look at it from the outside. If we'd been made to stay inside Bill's consciousness, this would have provided a convention which could have covered and justified the play's movement from naturalism into stylization and the change would have emerged as the result of tricks played by Bill's consciousness, not by the writer. But as usual Osborne tries to take in more than one action can digest and to do so he has to shift awkwardly between one viewpoint and another. From one angle, the trouble with Bill is that he is sinking into his own subjectivity; from his own point of view the trouble is that other people are withdrawing from him. From either vantage point, a good play could have been written, but not from both at the same time.

Unsuccessful as it is, *Inadmissible Evidence* is still the highest refinement Osborne has yet achieved on the technique of the one-man play. The telephone monologues are better, dramatically, than any of his other monologues and he makes a brave attempt to locate the bounds of the central character's solipsism. For the first time he highlights isolation as the subject, not leaving it just as an undefined condition of the hero's life, as it was with Luther's. But as with Jack Oakham in *The World of Paul Slickey*, it's impossible to bring a central character into critical focus just by using his own vision. It could have been done through the vision of other characters like Hudson and Joy, as to some extent it is, but there's a rift between the two groups of minor characters. Hudson, Jones, Shirley, and Joy exist on a much more realistic level than the three divorce clients, Jane, the daughter, and the Liz of the final scene, who all seem to be partly real, partly projections of Bill's brain.

The naturalistic characters and the naturalistic parts of the action are the most successful. Osborne makes more use than ever before of background detail. We believe in the solicitor's office as a place where people work. Jocelyn Herbert's set helped a good deal, but the reality of the professional situation is developed mainly by Bill's scenes with his office staff, Hudson, Jones, Joy, and Shirley. More than in any other Osborne play, we have development and interaction of character here. The characters aren't presented in a single scene and then dropped, and they aren't developed in terms of self-revealing monologues. Hudson, particularly as played by Arthur Lowe at the Royal Court, is a subtle and sympathetic study of the conventional employee, tolerant of his boss's quirks but limited in his commitment. We are shown exactly the point up to which Bill can exploit Hudson, pushing the routine work on to him, depending on him for the smooth running of the office, and exactly the point at which he imposes too much. Emotional reassurance is what Hudson refuses to give, can't afford to give, and even the offer of a partnership isn't enough to buy this, which is what Bill most desperately needs. Jones, the younger solicitor, is less interesting to Osborne, as he is to Bill, but the scenes with him are well done, especially the final one when Bill tries to test his loyalty and of course finds it limited. Jones cannot be relied on either.

> BILL: If Mr. Hudson leaves, do you think you could take his place?
> JONES: I don't know. I might.
> BILL: But you might not. You might go elsewhere?
> JONES: Well, I haven't had a lot of experience yet, and it doesn't do any harm to strike out a bit—
> BILL: That's right. I think you should.

The two girls are equally well drawn. Shirley's brewing anger is built up both when she's on stage and when she's off, until it explodes and she strikes back in the only way she can at the man who has used her—by leaving. She'll need money for the baby she's going to have and she could easily have gone on working for five or six months, but it's more important to get her revenge, such as it is. Osborne finds just the right details for recrimination and just the right tone of voice.

> One week-end in Leicester on client's business. Two week-ends in Southend on client's business. Moss Mansions—remember them? Four days in Hamburg on client's business. One crummy client's flat in Chiswick. And three times on *this* floor.

At first Joy's sugar is contrasted with Shirley's vinegar. She's the girl who shows sympathy and brings him his glass of water and lets him make love to her on the office floor and obeys all his curt orders over the intercom. But with her too, the moment of withdrawal comes.

> What do you want me to do? Press myself in a book for you? You know what? I think they're all right. I don't like you either.

So she decides to take the day off tomorrow.

> I've not been feeling so good lately. I think maybe I need a bit of a rest.

This works well. The withdrawal doesn't come across as just another predictable piece of the pattern in which everybody is withdrawing from Bill. Joy's reaction seems the natural outcome of the way we've seen her treated.

Inadmissible Evidence could be a turning point for Osborne. Of all his plays, it's the one which brings his problems as a playwright into the clearest focus. More than anything else, they are problems of integration: how to integrate the stylistic experiments into one style which is that of the whole play, dovetailing the more stylized scenes with the more realistic scenes; how to integrate the monologue into dialogue and action; how to integrate the hero into the body of the play. He solved the problem of realism and stylization in the first two acts of *The Entertainer*, but he's never repeated the success since. He's made monologues work very well in Bill Maitland's telephone conversations, but he doesn't seem to realize the implications of his own discovery that they succeed best when there's no on-stage audience. And stubbornly though he struggles to make the hero's subjectivity into the subject of *Inadmissible Evidence*, he must surely have come to realize, during the course of writing it, that one man's consciousness can only be examined as an object if it's examined from outside. If he doesn't go on to solve these problems now, after his experience in *Inadmissible Evidence*, then he never will.

A Bond Honoured

It was Kenneth Tynan who commissioned Osborne to adapt Lope de Vega's *La Fianza Satisfecha* for the National Theatre. It's a play with a great deal in it that could be expected to appeal to him. Leonido, the villainous hero, not only has long speeches of invective which translate effectively into Jimmy Porterese but he sets himself up as a solo fighter against all the values of his age. His life is "dedicated to the destruction of honour."* His object is "to insult the blood that flows in his veins," to disgrace his family and all it stands for, and to show that nothing human or superhuman can stop him. Before the action starts, he has seduced "many a delicious body," beaten a priest in front of his own altar, and killed his mother, after trying to rape her. In the course of the action, boasting that God will pay all his debts and that he will settle up with Him later, he tries to rape his sister on her wedding night, slashes her and her bridegroom on the face with his

* My quotations are taken from Joe Burroughs's translation, which was first broadcast on the Third Programme in December 1966.

sword, humiliates, insults and finally blinds his father, and renounces his religion to dress as a Moor.

Osborne approaches the text with relish but without reverence:

> It was in three acts, had an absurd plot, some ridiculous characters and some very heavy humour. What did interest me was the Christian framework of the play and the potentially fascinating dialectic with the principal character. So I concentrated on his development (in the original he rapes his sister in the opening moments of the play without any preparatory explanation of his character or circumstances) and discarded most of the rest, reducing the play to one long act.
> *A Bond Honoured* is the result.

This is not only inaccurate on the minor point that in Lope, Leonido doesn't succeed in raping Marcela —in Osborne's version he has made love to her many times—but misleading on a major point: in reality, Osborne discards comparatively little. He tightens and prunes the play, blowing the dust out of Lope's antiquated language, paring down the soliloquies and set speeches, and he does valuable work in translating narrative into action. But although things happen much faster in Osborne's version, the same things happen. He even keeps the far-fetched moment of discovery at the end of the play, which saves the beautiful Lidora at the last moment from having to marry the Moorish King Berlebeyo. His henchman, Zulema, suddenly produces a letter which was entrusted to him by the king's dying father, who had left instructions that Berlebeyo must read it before being betrothed. The letter reveals that Lidora is not a Moor but a Christian whom the old king rescued from the mouth of a she-bear when he was hunting on the shores of Alicarte in Sicily. Only a moment ago, we have heard from Leonido how his mother gave birth to two babies in a field just before he killed her, and how the first of these was carried off by a bear. So Lidora is Marcela's long-lost twin sister.

But Osborne goes even further. In Lope, both Leonido's attempts at incest fail. In Osborne, he succeeds not only with his sister, but with his mother, who hardly resists, and Marcela, his sister, is also his daughter. In John Dexter's production at the National Theatre, the strain on our credulity was increased still further by our having to accept Janina Faye and Maggie Smith as twin sisters, and Robert Stephens as the father of both of them. We also had to try not to be distracted by the semi-circle of actors sitting in semi-darkness and looking on at the rest of the action, and the pseudo-Japanese swordplay—with stylized swipes and dodges and a red scarf thrown about the victim's face to denote blood—often made it impossible to know whether he was meant to be wounded or killed.

But it's hard to see how anything could have been made out of Lope's play that would have much meaning for a contemporary English audience. Theatrically, there is a great potential interest in the figure of a hero who pursues evil in an almost saintly way, like Genet, using his own life as a laboratory test to locate the bounds of human possibility, but Lope's terms of reference are so very different from ours. In Spain, three hundred and fifty years ago, much of the play's meaning must have hinged on the question of when and how God would take his revenge on this "gluttony of disdain—disdain of God and Man." "God in Heaven and the Devil in Hell are impotent before me," Leonido boasts to King Berlebeyo, "and I pray God, infidel, that you have brought Hell along with you for its very devils burn to see more of my prowess." It would have meant much more to a Spanish audience then to see a Christian voluntarily dressing as a Moor, and Lope's text, unlike Osborne's, is quite unambiguous in identifying the poor shepherd with Christ. When Leonido calls him "a barefoot, hangdog fool walking on thorns and moaning maudlin pieties," the answer is

> My condition is an earnest of your debt to me. You owe me your life and you must pay me your life.

Leonido binds him with a rope that he finds in his pack, but the pack is so heavy that Leonido can hardly lift it.

> It is the weight of all your sins. A weight I have long borne for you.

In Lope's play, when Christ rebukes him for mocking his cross, Leonido recognizes him and is terrified. In Osborne's play, Leonido threatens the shepherd.

> Why are you mocking me? If you were God himself, you'd get no reprieve from me. I am going to kill you.
> (*He falls to the ground.*)

And when he recognizes that he is confronted at last with his creditor, his reaction, like that of the little man in Archie Rice's story about Judgment Day, is a refusal to be awed.

> I am overspent. It's not in your interest to believe me. But it is the case. I always knew it would be so. You will get, if you are so fortunate, a bankrupt's farewell, which is somewhat less than a

penny in the pound. So be it then. You will have had access to my books, so there is nothing for me to do but acknowledge each item, which might give satisfaction to you as a kind of divine lawyer's fee, but as wearisome to me as the hell I go to and the hell I came from. You shall have my life, which is what you came for. It's no more than fluff at the bottom of the pocket. (*Gives him fluff.*)

The shepherd answers, like the saint in Archie Rice's story, with pleasure and acceptance.

Let me embrace you.

But Leonido refuses.

Kill me first.
(*The shepherd goes.*)
I'll go to such extremes the world will use me as an example.

Lope's Leonido repents and prays; Osborne's Leonido wants to be judged.

We don't expect acquittal do we? Perhaps *they* do though. He looked uncertain. No, we want a harsh tribunal and the full exercise of justice.

This gives him a superficial resemblance to Camus's Meursault in *L'Etranger* or to the penitent judge in *La Chute* but Osborne's Leonido is less of an existentialist hero—and less of a solipsist than Lope's.

You would have uprooted everything; for to destroy was to you to create. You knew no curb; to offend others was to vindicate yourself. You stood against all proven belief; all true virtue, because in your conceit you believed that nothing outside yourself existed or was worthy of existence.

Osborne might have written a better play if he had made this his starting point and made more of an effort to define Leonido's solipsism in terms of his relationships with the other characters, including Christ. As it is, he loosens the screws in the Christian framework of Lope's play and his version is much more of a one-man play than the original. Leonido becomes a bore because he has no real opposition. The other characters are all foils and pasteboard butts.

Most of the new writing that Osborne has done comes at the beginning of the play in the scene with Tizon, the servant, and with Marcela. Marcela, vacillating between consent and resistance, certainly comes to life more than she does in Lope, but the opening scene with Tizon, which Osborne tricks out to four times its original length—in order to write in a preparatory explanation of Leonido's character and circumstances—gets the play off to a very bad start. It imposes an impossible burden on the actor playing Leonido, who has to move restlessly round the stage in circles, explaining his motives to his servant at the same time as he is venting his anger on him. Inevitably, Robert Stephens seemed to be moving too much, working up an energy which he was having to impose from outside on the situation, constantly threatening and shouting at a wretch you felt he wouldn't have wasted so much breath on. But if Tizon is inadequate as a victim, so are all the others—the flimsy father, the dull bridegroom, and the unconvincing Moors. If only Tynan had given him a play to translate which didn't have a central character that towered above everybody else.

Time Present
AND
The Hotel in Amsterdam

Osborne's original intention was to put on *Time Present* and *The Hotel in Amsterdam* together with a modern version of *Coriolanus* set in an African republic. The three plays were to be presented "almost in the manner of a retrospective exhibition. Or, at least, as a near to mid-way pause." *Coriolanus* was abandoned but *Time Present* opened at the Royal Court at the end of May 1968 with Osborne's wife, Jill Bennett, in the lead, followed by *The Hotel in Amsterdam* at the beginning of July with Paul Scofield in the lead. Both transferred to the West End, where they ran simultaneously.

What was most disappointing about them was a total lack of the energy that had made the earlier plays so exciting. Again the minor characters—which is to say all the characters except one—are there to link the leading character's monologues together and to listen to them, but neither play has monologues in it that can compare with the monologues in *Look Back in Anger* or *The Entertainer*. They are less abrasive and less funny but what matters even more is that, instead of being committed to a way of living,

113

they are only committed to a way of feeling.

In an interview with Kenneth Tynan in the *Observer*,* Osborne said: "I think one prejudice is worth twenty principles." He would not have said that in 1956. Jimmy Porter certainly had prejudices but he believed in them as if they were principles. Pamela in *Time Present* may not have withdrawn into her private life as totally as Laurie in *The Hotel in Amsterdam*. She still pontificates about politics and social life in the country as a whole. But she speaks with an unmistakably private voice and the whole effort of the play is to push her way of feeling at us as the right one.

She is highly articulate, not to say vociferous, about her attitudes. Much of what she says is likely to lose sympathy for her, and to counterbalance this the situation is contrived to win as much sympathy as possible. She is an actress, talented but out of work. In Act One, her actor father, Sir Gideon Orme, who sounds more or less like Sir Donald Wolfit, is dying in the hospital and she is taking turns with her mother sitting at his bedside. But she does not repeat Jimmy Porter's experience of watching someone dying. On hearing over the telephone that he is dead she refuses to go to the hospital, but her attempt to continue a conversation she is having about him provides a cue for a breakdown which repeats the technique of Archie Rice's breakdown over his two nuns story. This is followed rapidly by the curtain.

In Act Two, some weeks later, she is pregnant by a playwright who is now having an affair with her best friend, a Labour M.P., whose flat she is sharing. The man is so spineless and she is so strong that she could easily get him back if she wanted to, but she doesn't. Without telling him that she is pregnant,

* June 30, and July 7, 1968.

she phones her agent in his presence to ask for the name of an abortionist, arranging to move into the agent's flat (he is a Jewish homosexual) until the operation.

She also has to suffer in Act Two during a visit from Abigail, a successful rival actress, who, like Vanessa Redgrave, makes speeches about Cuba. Abigail is so carried away by the success of the play she has just opened in that she has forgotten to go to Orme's memorial service where she was meant to be reading one of the lessons. In Act One we had several monologues abusing her roundly, almost as if she were a female Brother Nigel. In her presence we do not even get a dramatic confrontation. As with the bereavement and the pregnancy, Pamela suffers in silence.

But the bid for sympathy comes rather too late: her behavior in Act One must have put most of the audience irretrievably against her. Neither her mother, Edith, nor her stepsister, Pauline, is particularly sympathetic or particularly real. But Pamela is strenuously and gratuitously offensive to them and to Constance (the M.P.). Pauline, like Bill Maitland's daughter in *Inadmissible Evidence*, is designed as a representative of London's youth. This sequence comes while Pamela is pouring out champagne:

> PAMELA: I won't offer you any, Pauline. She doesn't approve of alcohol, do you? Haven't got any L.S.D. to offer you.
> PAULINE: Thanks, Pamela. I think I will have a glass.
> PAMELA: Oh, good. Unless Constance has got some pot upstairs. Didn't your lover leave his tin behind the last time? There! Nothing vulgar. Just good trusty old Moet. Her lover drinks nothing but Dom Perignon. Very vulgar. Oh, that's better.

(*To Constance.*) Did you vote or divide or whatever? (*She nods.*) Don't tell me—you won. What
were the figures?

CONSTANCE: 245–129.

PAMELA: Surprise. Like playing for matches really
isn't it? (*To Pauline.*) I suppose that hippie outside belongs to you?

EDITH: Who?

PAMELA: Does he have a name or is he a group? It
was a bit difficult to tell if he was one or several.

PAULINE: You know perfectly well.

EDITH: Did you bring Dave, darling?

PAULINE: He doesn't mind waiting.

EDITH: You should have brought him up.

PAMELA: No, she was quite right.

PAULINE: He's O.K., Mummy. He said he'd come
with us.

EDITH: You know Pamela.

PAMELA: Well enough. Anyway, Constance has just
had her nice carpet cleaned.

PAULINE: So what are you supposed to be proving?

PAMELA: I'm just enjoying my first drink of the
evening.

PAULINE: Just bitchy and you know it.

PAMELA: You see, you really don't know me. But no
loss. For either of us.

EDITH: Are you sure you haven't had a drink?

PAMELA: I told you.

EDITH: You do seem—a bit exhilarated.

PAMELA: I walked through the side streets. No Andrew.

EDITH: I shouldn't stay up, Pamela.

PAMELA: *You've* never been an actor. One needs to
wind down.

PAULINE: Have you been performing then?

PAMELA: No, but my papa has. You don't think
someone will tow Dave away if you leave him?

PAULINE: Oh, you're a drag—

PAMELA: Looks pretty high to me.

EDITH: What's the matter with him?

PAMELA: He's on what your children call a trip,
Mama. Having unmemorable visions in a psyche-
delic, sort of holiday camp shirt and a raccoon
coat in my doorway. Trip clothes, right, Pauline?

> PAULINE: You just hate any sort of fun or anything.
> PAMELA: Give him the trip home, will you, darling?
> And I don't think it's much fun taking Dave,
> Dave for an all night rave in hospital, so just get
> your skates on will you and get rid of him?

As Irving Wardle said in *The Times,* the difference between this sort of thing and Jimmy Porter's assaults on Nigel is that Pamela never seems to have met the enemy in person, only to have read about him in the newspapers.

Jimmy Porter's invective was good enough for us not to need more than a minimal dramatic situation, but loose writing like this fails to distract us from the loose and clumsy construction. The play opens with a very awkward exposition scene in which Edith and Pauline—whose own characters are not going to be developed at all—sit in armchairs and have a protracted conversation from which we are meant to absorb a lot of information about the situation and about characters we have not met. When Pamela finally arrives, her rudeness provides tension of a sort but when she is left alone with Constance, there is no tension at all, only a flabby conversation.

> PAMELA: You looked as if the entire Cabinet was lin-
> ing up for you. They should be grateful you don't
> look like that woman—what is she, in the Treas-
> ury—the one with the teeth?
> CONSTANCE: I wouldn't mind being as bright as she
> is.
> PAMELA: I wouldn't mind if she were as pretty as
> you.
> CONSTANCE: I don't think you should judge by ex-
> ternals so much.
> PAMELA: I've just a superficial manner, often saying
> serious things. Which is the other way round to
> people like her. Just because she's got a double
> first in P.P.E. or I.T.V., there's no reason why

she shouldn't get her teeth fixed. That's arrogance and self-deception. Perhaps that's why she's a big wheel in the Party.

CONSTANCE: I think she's a nice woman, really, shy and, yes, well a bit serious, but a first rate mind.

PAMELA: Um. Well, you know her. I find it hard to believe she's really wise to inflict those green teeth on people. Sort of autumnal teeth, aren't they? That should make her shy but she's not. I think someone must have told her once she looked like a tiger and she's been flashing them at you behind that crimped up seaweed she thinks is a serious politician's hair-do ever since. Is it a wig?

CONSTANCE: No. Poor woman. We can't all look like film stars.

PAMELA: Well, perhaps she should, poor dear. How can you be really intelligent and be satisfied with that? It's obviously all a great production number. Even if she does feel she's got unfair competition with the men.

CONSTANCE: It isn't easy, Pamela. It's easier in your line.

This is only very mildly amusing and it contributes nothing to either character or situation. The character of Constance is embarrassingly unsatisfactory. She is so feeble it is impossible to believe that anyone would vote for her, and she is made to grovel tiresomely and at considerable length in an attempt to convince us that Pamela is a worthwhile person.

CONSTANCE: It's as if you hate what I do, what I am, everything about me. I know a lot of it seems funny and wasted effort but a lot of effort *is* funny and wasted.

PAMELA: I don't mind effort. I'm not so keen on strain.

CONSTANCE: You make me feel very shabby and inept and all thumbs sometimes.

PAMELA: *I* do! But, Constance, I don't . . . I don't know anything I'm ever talking about except for odd things. I'm almost totally ignorant, you know that.

CONSTANCE: No, you're not. You're very perceptive.

PAMELA: I'm not perceptive. I'm just full of bias. *And* I'm uneducated. I went to about twenty expensive schools and I never learnt anything in any of them. Except to play tennis.

CONSTANCE: You know how I admire you and what you do.

PAMELA: But I have never done anything very memorable. How can you?

CONSTANCE: I know you have formidable qualities . . .

PAMELA: Even if they haven't been exploited yet?

CONSTANCE: I respect and admire you for what you are.

PAMELA: I respect and admire you.

CONSTANCE: I don't think so. I wish you did.

PAMELA: It shouldn't matter to you.

CONSTANCE: Well, it does. Your good opinion is important to me. More so than most of the people I deal with. I know we inhabit different worlds, but they're not really so different always. And also, I thought that we were, were very much alike you and I.

One reviewer thought that the main theme of the play was the latent Lesbian relationship between the two women. The lack of definition in the writing is such that it is impossible to be certain that he is wrong, except that to talk of themes implies much more control and clear articulation than in fact there is.

Altogether the relationship between Constance, Pamela and Murray, the playwright, remains very obscure—mainly, I think, because Osborne has not taken enough trouble with it. Quite apart from his failure to make Murray into a man who could engage Pamela in anything more serious than a casual conversation when there was no one more interesting around, her behavior over the pregnancy seems very unresolved, even allowing for the possibility that she may be ambivalent over whether or not she wants him to know that he is the father of her child. Neither the telephone conversation with the agent nor her talk of borrowing money from Murray has the effect of making him even entertain the possibility that he might be the father, and instead of bringing his spinelessness into focus, the scene ebbs into another monologue:

> MURRAY: You can't be serious about Ladies' Services?
>
> PAMELA: My dear, it's like going to the crimpers. Only more expensive. I may have to borrow some money from you.
>
> MURRAY: I'll give it to you, of course.
>
> PAMELA: You'll lend it to me. No, you won't. I'll borrow it from Bernard. I owe him enough already, but never mind.
>
> MURRAY: You must.
>
> PAMELA: I mustn't anything. I'd go to Wee Willie Wonder—
>
> MURRAY: Wee who?
>
> PAMELA: Wee Willie Wonder. My gynaecologist. But he'd only give me a lecture. Oh, he'd do it.
>
> MURRAY: Is he a moralist too?
>
> PAMELA: Not he. He's not one of those bear down and be joyful queens. He'd just lecture me.
>
> MURRAY: What about?
>
> PAMELA: Like you, like Mama and Constance. Except that he knows me better. Anyway, he's a nice sensitive man. He'll worry about me and reproach himself and I'll have him coming round to the house.
>
> MURRAY: How did it happen?
>
> PAMELA: What? Oh, guess.
>
> MURRAY: Has it . . . ?
>
> PAMELA: No, it's never happened before. At least I've not dried up like an old prune after all. You've proved that. That should please you. Still,

> even Wee Willie nods sometimes. And it's a mys-
> terious, capricious place in there. Especially
> mine. Not surprising. It feels like a Bosch trip-
> tych often enough. It's been better lately, I
> thought it was odd.
>
> MURRAY: What do you mean: that should please
> you?
>
> PAMELA: Oh, your eyes. Not just now. I used to see
> it in my previous gentleman's face sometimes—
> before he left me. When he was making love to
> me. He never said anything. He was too reticent.
> I suppose it's a question of if you become literally
> substantial they can luxuriate in their abstraction
> with a nice trailing guide line to mother earth.
> Trailing guide line, I've said that out of your
> play. There, you see, I read very carefully. Do
> go, Murray. I want to get undressed and I feel
> shy with you about the place and Constance will
> be back and it's quite clear you're longing to tell
> her.

The only explanation, I think, is that the play was
written far too quickly. In the *Observer* interview,
when Tynan questioned Osborne about his refusal to
revise his plays once they were finished, this was his
answer:

> I suppose it's just arrogance, but I've always
> thought that ultimately I know best. That's why
> George Devine was such a sheet-anchor for me. He
> would put the case to you for cutting out the things
> that made people yawn, but ultimately he would
> stand by your judgement. Because he thought that
> was what mattered. Your private wound was more
> important than somebody else's public satisfaction.

He wrote *Look Back in Anger* in nine days and *The
Entertainer* in eleven, but at that time, apparently,
his private wounds could be teased into a public sig-
nificance far more readily. There is a great deal in

Time Present that ought to have been cut, but the weaknesses could not be cured merely by cutting.

Whatever he may say about his indifference to whether his audience is satisfied or not, in writing plays for it, Osborne is obviously trying to communicate with it. The question is whether he is trying to communicate through the play form or through individual speeches, writing the rest of the play merely as a frame for them. The truth about *Time Present* is that he seems only superficially concerned about the situation and the relationships. What interests him is what Pamela feels—about hippies and drug-taking, about lady novelists, about lady politicians and the Labour Party, about actors like Orme-Wolfit and actresses like Abigail-Vanessa and so on and so on. And these feelings derive with an undisguised directness from Osborne's own feelings about hippies and drug-taking, lady politicians, etc., etc. In other words, more than any of his previous plays *Time Present* seems to be aspiring towards the condition of an interview.

This is also true of *The Hotel in Amsterdam*, in which most of the space is taken up by letting the minor characters give very brief answers to questions like "do you ever wake up with an awful burn in the stomach?" which are posed by Laurie, who then answers himself at much greater length. They then prime him with questions and comments which encourage him to develop his answer at still greater length:

> LAURIE: I'm afraid I usually need a drink. It's the only thing that burns it out. Need to weld my guts with a torch. Then about nine, it eases off. I read the post. Try to put off work. Have a so-

called business lunch. That's a good waste of time. Then I know I'll have to sleep in the afternoon.

AMY: Does Margaret get up when you're like that?

LAURIE: She can't—poor old thing. You see she can't get off to sleep. So by the time I'm about to totter about downstairs, reading last night's evening papers, she's only just managed to get off. Especially now.

AMY: When she's pregnant?

(Laurie motions her silent at the word.)

LAURIE: So, I'm afraid we're a bit out of step with sleep. When I was eighteen I used to sleep fourteen hours on Sundays. When my mother would let me.

DAN: My mother made too much noise.

LAURIE: If *only* you can find enough energy. Where do you find it? Where's the spring?

AMY: You're loaded with it. You've got far more than Dan.

LAURIE: No, I haven't. Dan doesn't need energy. He runs perfectly efficiently on paraffin oil. You fill him up once a year and he's alight for another twelve months. With me, I need the super quality high-thing stuff poured into my tank twice a day. Look at K.L. He's unstoppable, you never have to wind him up. He just goes. Like that.

AMY: He gets very worn out.

LAURIE: I should think he does. If I did what he does in a day, I'd be in bed for a month.

DAN: He delegates.

LAURIE: Ah, yes—the operator's alchemy. Where do you get it? He takes it from *us*. We could be giving it to one another. He's been draining our tanks, filling his own. Filling up on all of us, splitting us up.

Certainly, it is a better play than *Time Present*, with fewer patches of boredom and a more likable hero. Paul Scofield made the very most of the set pieces, particularly the nonsensical improvisation in bad Italian, the imaginary "thank you" letter from a poor relation acknowledging a money gift, and the declaration of love to Gus's wife, Annie, while sitting not quite next to her on the sofa, without making a move to touch her. But though the character profited from the performance, it by no means depended parasitically on it—there is great charm in the writing. The monologues are quieter, less vindictive and on the whole shorter than those of any other Osborne hero, but much better written and much wittier than Pamela's.

The situation is again minimal. Laurie and his wife, Margaret, have come to Amsterdam with two other couples mainly to escape for a long weekend from K.L., the tyrant film producer who overshadows their normal lives. Gus is his film editor and Amy is his secretary. Dan is her husband. They all sit about talking in the drawing room of a suite in the hotel. There are some conversations about practicalities like tipping the porter, ordering drinks, and deciding which restaurant to have dinner in, but most of the chat is geared to a pseudo-interview of Laurie.

The only other character to emerge with any definition is Gus. His character may not develop, but at least we know what he is like—fussy, kindly, anxious to please, nervous, compulsive about making plans in advance and unable to say whether he wants a drink until he has consulted Annie. But she, Margaret, and Dan, a painter, are all very shadowy and Amy is just a stereotype of the highly efficient secretary of a high-powered boss.

Apart from involving English couples in a foreign hotel, what makes the play so reminiscent of Noel Coward is the self-congratulatory tone of the conversation. The characters are delighted with themselves for being so likable and for liking each other so much. They preen themselves on having escaped from K.L. and they hope that Margaret's sister, Gillian, will not join them.

> LAURIE: What did you go and tell your bloody sister we were here for?
>
> MARGARET: Oh, don't be silly. I told her not to tell anyone we're here.
>
> LAURIE: But what did you tell her *for?* She's not one of us.
>
> MARGARET: Isn't she?
>
> LAURIE: Well, she's not really anything to do with K.L. And, besides, she wouldn't like it. She thinks we're all a bit flippant and middle-aged. Not half as middle-aged as her.
>
> MARGARET: Come on. You like her. It's just that she's been having a bad time lately.
>
> LAURIE: What bad time?
>
> MARGARET: I'm not sure. But this affair she's having—
>
> LAURIE: Oh, fleecing another rich duke of £500 and clenching her fists because she didn't lose her cherry until she was twenty-eight and she doesn't think she gives satisfaction and she plays Bach fugues all night and doesn't wash her hair because it's all so difficult. Blimey! I think *I* complain. She needs a public recognition for the suffering she undergoes, that's all. Then she'll feel better. She should get the Golden Sanitary Towel Award. K.L. can give it to her at the Dorchester with all the past winners present.

Certainly this is hearteningly closer to Osborne's old style of humor, but it is only when Gillian arrives, nearly halfway through the second act, that we get any suspense or anything approaching a dramatic situation. Gillian is obviously in some dire emotional trouble and, as the stage direction tells us, "she has broken the fragile spell." But Osborne achieves a good variation of the Archie Rice breakdown technique. After she has made a valiant effort to fit in with the mood of the others, chattering as brightly as she can, Laurie releases her from the duty of going on trying:

Gillian, for Christ's sake burst into tears . . .

And slowly she crumples. Margaret takes her off into a bedroom, leaving us in suspenseful ignorance of what is upsetting her and after an amusingly protracted sequence in which Gus dithers before going out to leave Laurie alone with Annie, we get their throwaway love scene. This is good, though it comes far too late in the play to be capable of development. Not that Osborne is interested in developing it. But the dialogue he writes for them has a cutting edge which shows up just how undramatic most of the earlier dialogue is.

ANNIE: Have you been unfaithful to her?
LAURIE: Yes.
ANNIE: Enjoyable?
LAURIE: Not very.
ANNIE: Often?
LAURIE: No. Not inordinately.
ANNIE: When was the last time?
LAURIE: Six months. Just a few times.
ANNIE: Before that?
LAURIE: Not for ages.
ANNIE: What's ages?
LAURIE: When she was in the nursing home . . .
ANNIE: In the nursing home? You mean, not—
LAURIE: Yes.
ANNIE: I see.
LAURIE: Are you shocked?
ANNIE: No. Surprised . . . Not really.
LAURIE: I thought you might say: men!
ANNIE: You're not men! I'd better go and change.
LAURIE: Gus'll call you. Have some more . . . I've wanted to tell you.
ANNIE: Have you?

LAURIE: No one knows. You won't tell Gus, will you?

ANNIE: I won't tell anyone . . . Why did you want to tell me?

LAURIE: Why? Because . . . to me . . . you have always been the most dashing . . . romantic . . . friendly . . . playful . . . loving . . . impetuous . . . larky . . . fearful . . . detached . . . constant . . . woman I have ever met . . . and I love you . . . I don't know how else one says it . . . one shouldn't . . . and I've always thought you felt . . . perhaps . . . the same about me.

ANNIE: I do.

But we are altogether in a different convention now and in the last three minutes of the play we get more action than its frail structure can take. Coming out of the bedroom, Margaret says that Gillian nearly committed suicide over the weekend. Gillian, she says, has also told K.L. where they all are and a few seconds later the telephone rings with the news that K.L. has committed suicide—a moment which has its theatrical impact, of course, but forms a melodramatic and highly inept climax for a conversation play like this.

West of Suez

If all Osborne's plays aspire to the condition of the interview, *West of Suez* is the one in which this is more obvious than ever. The method of the play is very similar to that of *Hotel in Amsterdam*: a successful writer and a galaxy of supporting characters who in some way depend on him are placed in a foreign environment. Without trying very hard to focus it or them, or the effect it has on them, the action shows them reacting to it as the dialogue moves placidly along, recording their small talk. In effect, they interview each other throughout most of both plays, as in the leisurely scene which opens Act Two of *West of Suez* when Frederica, the most talkative of an English writer's four daughters, asks everyone on stage what he is thinking about.

There is very little shape or situation or action in either play, but, as if to compensate, both end with violence—an off-stage suicide in *Hotel in Amsterdam*, an on-stage killing in *West of Suez*. And the one scene in this play which is highly entertaining is actually an interview: Wyatt Gillman, an elderly writer, talks to a reporter from the island newspaper in the pres-

ence of most of the other characters; he turns out to
have a great many of the same predilections and
prejudices as Osborne himself, and the writing, which
is elsewhere rather flabby, suddenly becomes crisp
and spiky as interviewer and subject cross swords:

> WYATT: I am never patronizing. I am in no position
> to be so. And never have been.
>
> MRS. JAMES: How do you feel at the moment? How do
> you feel at the moment?
>
> WYATT: Just about the same as usual. Except hotter.
> Always weary, ineffably bored, always in some
> sort of vague pain and always with a bit of un-
> satisfying hatred burning away in the old inside
> like heartburn or indigestion.
>
> MRS. JAMES: I can see we may not get very far.
>
> WYATT: Does it matter?
>
> MRS. JAMES: Not to you. I've simply been sent to do
> a job. Well, let's take an easy one first: what do
> you think of your fellow writers?
>
> WYATT: Fellow writers! What a dreadful expression!
>
> MRS. JAMES: I'm sorry, I couldn't think of anything
> else to describe the people who practise the same
> profession.
>
> WYATT: I try not to think of my fellow writers. If
> they're better than I am, I am disturbed. If they're
> worse, which is unusual, I simply feel sorry.
>
> MRS. JAMES: What do you think of the state of Eng-
> lish literature at the moment?
>
> WYATT: Nothing at all.
>
> MRS. JAMES: Would you say that you strike postures
> with people whom you regard as provincials?
>
> WYATT: Very likely, I'm afraid. But not in your case.
> You're quite clearly very sophisticated. I mean,
> you wouldn't have much trouble getting the edge
> on me. You can never win an interview if you're
> being interviewed.
>
> MRS. JAMES: I'm not trying to win anything. I'm
> simply trying to arrive at some sort of approxima-
> tion of the truth.
>
> WYATT: Do you think there is such a thing?
>
> MRS. JAMES: I don't think you should ask me facile

questions, even if you are a famous man and paying us a visit.

WYATT: I'm not paying you a visit. I am visiting my
daughter and her husband. And staying with my
other daughter and friends.

MRS. JAMES: Do you think we should give up this
interview?

WYATT: I think that the onus is entirely upon you.

MRS. JAMES: Quite right. What do you think of as
being Utopia?

The mixture of attraction and revulsion that Osborne feels towards the interview situation helps to
produce a piquancy and a tension which become
highly theatrical. This atmosphere survives even
when the discursive questioning leads to pronounce-
ments about the direction art is currently going in
and to the airing of Osborne's familiar misgivings
about the critics.

There is nothing in the dialogue to give any sub-
stantiation to the assertion that Wyatt is a distin-
guished writer. Osborne needs him to be a celebrity
to justify the interview and the way everyone lion-
izes him; but the plot otherwise makes little use of
his presumed status as a writer, and his dialogue
could equally well have been written for a successful
businessman. There is no indication of literary flair
in it, or even of literary preoccupations.

Altogether the plotting and construction are flimsy
and haphazard. The island, which seems to be in the
West Indies, was formerly a British colony, and
Wyatt's eldest daughter lives there with her husband, a retired brigadier. Osborne evinces little interest in either of them or in what their lives are like.
Wyatt's father was a colonial administrator, we are
told, and Wyatt, as an unsuccessful young writer,
used to move around with him to his various postings.
All four of the daughters were therefore born at dif-

ferent outposts of the Empire. It may well have been Osborne's intention to make some sort of statement emerge out of the dissonances between the aging girls' reminiscences of the imperial past and the actualities of the unglamorous present. But while a lot remains buried, little emerges, and it is far too confused to add up to a statement.

What confused the London audiences most of all was the final climax, in which Wyatt is gunned down by two of the islanders. In so far as there is any preparation for this at all, it comes at the end of the interview, when Wyatt is asked what he feels about the island and the people he has met:

> All the good things I've seen on the island seem to be legacies of the British, the Spanish and the Dutch, particularly in the buildings and what's left of any proper dispensation of the law. As for the people, they seem to me to be a very unappealing mixture of hysteria and lethargy, brutality and sentimentality.

It can be inferred that Mrs. James has told the islanders what he thinks of them and that they identify him with colonists and oppressors.

The first half of the play is almost totally lacking in tension and piquancy. An examination of the script shows that Wyatt does not make his first appearance until the bottom of page 30, and there are only 75 pages in all. Osborne wrote the part for Sir John Gielgud, but it was played by Sir Ralph Richardson, who charmingly bulldozed over the audience's boredom. Reminiscing about his past, chatting about what it feels like to be old, or pondering about how much of a nuisance he was being to the others, he lit up the dialogue enough to make it look less static.

But the play starts with a very long and tedious conversation between Frederica and her husband. Frederica was played by Jill Bennett, who tried, as in *Time Present*, to make the character into a lovable wasp with a strong personality. Occasionally there are faint echoes of the wit of *Look Back in Anger*, as in the freewheeling conversation between Wyatt and Frederica that goes on for nearly eighteen pages before the youngest daughter, Mary, and her husband, Robert, put in an appearance. However, a lot of space is given to idle marital bickering and to preparatory mentions of characters we have not yet met. With some of them, like the Brigadier, the owner of the house in which they are all staying, physical materialization adds nothing to what has already been done in the dialogue to characterize them. This suggests that Osborne has no deep interest in any of them as characters. Like so many of the people in *The World of Paul Slickey*—both those who appear and those who are only talked about—they are there only as representatives of something Osborne does not like, created only as butts for his satire. He uneconomically introduces seventeen characters into *West of Suez* (excluding walk-ons), but Wyatt and Frederica are the only two with whom he concerns himself deeply or sympathetically.

The strain in the relationship between Frederica and her husband, the surly resentfulness of the native waiter, Leroi, and the confrontation between Wyatt and another English writer, Lamb, are all subjects which could have been developed into situations, but Osborne seems interested neither in creating the kind of tension on which conventional theater depends, nor in offering any alternative to it. Sometimes one of the characters says something interesting or expresses himself in an arresting way, but whereas Pinter—even in the most desultory conversations he lets his characters embark on—preserves a tension, a stylishness, and an air of having one or two trump cards up his sleeve, Osborne lets the tension go so slack and the language become so dull that we welcome even small and diluted doses of Jimmy Porterishness:

> FREDERICA: I'd have got on the nearest dog-sled to the South Pole to get away from one more Christmas with that old gangster. Complaining, and wailing and scheming, impossible to please. Like having an incontinent, superannuated Mafia in your sitting room all day.

This is a description of her mother-in-law.

Things become a little more entertaining when Wyatt appears, but without the pressure of a situation the only way his personality can emerge is through self-display. Even before the interview, he therefore talks as if he were answering questions put by an imaginary interviewer. The other characters are made to play in with this, feeding him with the same sort of questions an interviewer might:

> ROBERT: What school did you go to?
> WYATT: Marlborough. That was *my* Western Front. Perhaps it wasn't so bad, though all the ones I've spoken to who were there then who say they were happy are the most awful types. Overweaning little swots or thumping great Prussian sons of Great Albion. All become florid M.P.'s or sarky tongued bullies at the bar; clammy old bishops and archbishops or those huge surgeons who tower over you in green and rubber wellies and call their patients "the meat." Of course I was the only one who didn't go to Eton. My father went, so did all my elder brothers.
> CHRISTOPHER: Why was that?

It would be an interesting if rather irritating experiment to calculate what percentage of the lines in the play could fairly be described as dressed-up answers to the inexhaustible question "What does Osborne dislike?" Some of the answers are hardly even dressed up. For example, there is one sequence where they all sit around discussing whom they would most like to send to the moon, and so get rid of.

What puts all this into an even stranger perspective is the revelation that chatter is one of the things Osborne dislikes. He makes Wyatt say:

> Birds chatter and *that* is their mortal flaw. Chatter sins against language and when we sin against the word, we sin against God. Gosh, I am pompous.

It may be that by now Osborne feels capable of playing such sophisticated games with the critics that he deliberately sews into the lining of a play a stick with which he is inviting them to beat it over the head, or it may be that he sees no relevance between this condemnation of chatter and the staple dialogue of the play.

Apart from this one remark of Wyatt's, the only suggestion of a set of values or a caliber of language different from that of the chatterers comes in a speech by a young character called Jed. Most of the chatterers are middle-aged or elderly. There is a young homosexual hairdresser, who is also a chatterer; the only other youngster is Jed, who is in his early twenties and has shoulder-length black hair. He is brought in by the hairdresser, Alastair:

> ALASTAIR: This is Jed. He's a student. He's just on his way.
> WYATT: How do you do, Jed. Where are you on your way to?
> JED: Wherever.

This is the only word Jed speaks until just before the final shooting, when he launches abruptly into a venomous tirade attacking all of them:

All I see, and I laugh when I see it, man, I laugh, is you pigs barbecued, barbecued in your own shit. *We're*, yes, we're going to take over and don't you begin to forget it. Man, I feel real sorry for your lot. No I don't . . . You got it coming. And you *have soon*. Think of the theatre of the mind, baby, old moulding babies, except you won't. We count and we *do*, not like you, we *really*, really do . . . Why we fall about laughing at you people, not people, you're not people, you pigs. We are people. *We* are. But not you. You don't understand and why should you because, believe me babies, old failing babies, words, yes I mean words, even what I'm saying to you now, is going to be the first to go. Go, baby. Go. You can't even make love. Do you understand one word, those old words you love so much, what I mean? No. And you won't. If it ain't written down, you don't believe it . . . There's only one word left and you know what that is. It's fuck, man. Fuck . . . That's the last of the English for you babies. Or maybe shit. Because that's what we're going to do on you. Shit. That's what you'll all go down in. One blissful, God-like shit. You think we're mother-fucking, stinking, yelling, shouting shits. Well that's what we are, babies. And there's nothing, not nothing you or anybody else can do about it. Jesus is sort of shit. But you're not even *shit*. We think, we fuck and we shit and that's what we do and you're on the great gasping end of it. Because you're pigs. Just take one little look at yourselves. You're pigs, babies. Pigs. And we're gonna shit you out of this world, babies.

Embarrassing, crude and repetitive though this is, it does have a force which is lacking in all the other dialogue. The most charitable interpretation of the play would be that Osborne created the chatter only to destroy it. Jed's speech probably gets as near to illiteracy as it is possible to get in a speech of this length in a play of this kind. However, if Osborne shares Jed's belief that the word, as such, is moribund and if the whole play is deliberately built as flimsily as a house of cards just for Jed to blow it down in one malevolent puff, all that can be said is that the point Osborne is trying to make cannot be made in these terms. The play's structure is simply too old-fashioned.

Of course Jed also has roots in Osborne's earlier plays and in the notorious "Damn you England" letter. Even the phrase about pigs barbecued in their own shit is reminiscent of the phrase "as you fry in your democratically elected hot-seats,"* and the attitude, like the whole tone, is remarkably similar. Jed is also being used as a spokesman for a whole age group, just as in *Inadmissible Evidence* Bill's daughter is made representative of her whole generation. The difference is that she listens to her father's attack on it without ever saying a word, while Jed harangues the others without ever having a word said to him in reply.

His speech comes at a climacteric moment in the action and it culminates, slightly out of character, in a very curious pronouncement:

> Colonialism is the fornication of the twentieth century. You can't be young. So all you'd better do, all you *will* do, is die, die, baby. And pretty damn soon. Just real soon. Like tomorrow. Or even tonight.

A minute later Wyatt is dead, shot by two natives. The point Osborne is trying to make about colonialism is far too muddled and generalized to emerge effectively from this bald linking of Jed's speech with

---

* See page 12.

the action of the islanders. Instead of being resolved, Osborne's old ambivalence about British imperialism, which appeared in the early plays like *Look Back in Anger* and *The Entertainer*, is getting in the way and merging with a similar ambivalence about the generation gap. Jed is not made at all attractive as a character, and Wyatt is given considerable charm; but it is clear that Osborne, like Jed, feels that the older generation has been allowed to "get away with it" for far too long and that the idea of retribution is not altogether unwelcome in his mind. Properly exploited this ambivalence could be quite valuable, but Osborne is still writing so self-indulgently that on present showing it is doubtful whether he will ever discover the right dramatic form to express it effectively.

CONCLUSION

"I want to make people feel," Osborne
wrote in *Declaration*,* "to give them lessons in feeling. They can think afterwards." It is the strength
of his own feelings that charge so many moments of
naked emotion in his plays with the power they have
to make an unforgettable impact—Kenneth Haigh's
breathless, feverish incredulity when Jimmy Porter
returned from the funeral to find that Alison had
just walked out on him, Olivier's breakdown in the
middle of the two nuns story, Nicol Williamson's
growing panic when the barrister's managing clerk
wouldn't speak to him over the telephone. But in the
early plays private anger frothed into public-spirited
indignation. In raging at Alison's behavior, Jimmy
Porter was hitting out at behavior which he saw as
typical of the ruling classes. When he broke down
after hearing that his son had been killed, Archie
Rice was weeping for all the powerless victims of the
irresponsible and incompetent politicians. And Bill

* *Declaration*, published by MacGibbon and Kee in 1957,
contained credos by Kenneth Tynan, John Osborne, John Wain,
Lindsay Anderson, Doris Lessing, Colin Wilson and the two
friends of his he made fashionable at that time—Stuart Holroyd
and Bill Hopkins.

Maitland was panicking at his isolation partly because the fact was being driven home to him that there was no one up there—or anywhere else—to look after him. The father figures have all let us down. The waving hand from the golden coach has its fingers parted in a sign of derision.

Yet the fusion of personal and public elements in Osborne's plays was always incomplete and finally unsatisfactory. His concern with social issues existed oddly alongside his obsession with the One and his indifference to the Many, even when the One was set up as a representative of the Many, someone who felt for them vicariously. Talking of Planchon's productions of Marivaux, Kenneth Tynan said: "He gives you a picture of the society which is hidden beneath the text. The sub-text in Stanislavsky is psychological; in a Brechtian production the sub-text is social." In Osborne's plays there was never any social sub-text.

He wanted to give people lessons in feeling but was he ever prepared to find out what people were feeling? "Nobody can be very interested in my contribution to a problem like the kind of houses people should have built for them," he wrote in *Declaration*, "the kind of school they should send their children to, or the pensions they should be able to look forward to. But there are other questions to be asked— how do people live inside those houses? What is their relationship with one another, and with their children, with their neighbours and the people across the street, or on the floor above? What are the things that are important to them, that make them care, give them hope and anxiety? What kind of language do they use to one another? What is the meaning of the work they do? Where does the pain lie? What are their expectations? What moves them, brings them together, makes them speak out? Where is the weakness, the loneliness? Where are the things that are unrealized? Where is the strength?" But even his early plays show very little evidence of interest in answering these questions, or in the effects that housing, schooling, and pensions have in conditioning feelings, language, work, and personal relationships.

If we ignore his influence on the English theater and concentrate on his achievement as a dramatist, what remains to be said? Apart from *Time Present*, all his plays have brilliant moments, but he has never yet maintained a consistency of style all through a play or a full control over the variations of tension and pressure. There must be a connection between his dislike of critics and the way he muzzles his self-critical faculties, as there obviously is between his dislike of revising and his weakness at constructing.

Irving Wardle has suggested that he has a hold on the theater-going public less as a dramatist than as a popular preacher, that the people who flocked to see *Time Present* and *The Hotel in Amsterdam* were less concerned with the quality of the plays than with the postures Osborne was adopting in them. This is probably true and possibly he could go on at least for a time writing bad plays which are good box-office draws. But it will be a terrible waste of an extraordinary talent if he goes on believing in inspiration and refusing to make himself into a good craftsman, as he probably could. With Jimmy Porter, Archie Rice and Bill Maitland, he succeeded brilliantly by pumping his own attitudes and phobias directly into the character. But if he goes on playing his impatient game of solitaire in which the cards have to come out right the first time or not at all, he may eventually find himself playing it alone.

He does not seem to be altogether unaware of this

danger. The desolation Bill Maitland feels in *Inadmissible Evidence* when deprived of social, sexual, and professional contacts, and even the island on which Wyatt Gillman ends his days in *West of Suez* could be seen as projections of a deep fear of isolation. The ultimate hell for Osborne would be a situation in which there was no one to ask him how he felt about things. But the more he tries to exorcise this terror by interviewing himself in his own plays, the more unlikely it becomes that he will ever commit himself fully to a discipline of writing in which he does his utmost to create full-blooded characters and then allow them to interact freely.

STAGE PRODUCTIONS

May 1956   *Look Back in Anger*, directed by
                    Tony Richardson, with Kenneth
                    Haigh and Alan Bates, at the Royal
                    Court.

April 1957   *The Entertainer*, directed by Tony
                    Richardson, with Sir Laurence Oliv-
                    ier and Brenda de Banzie, at the
                    Royal Court.

February 1958   *Epitaph for George Dillon*, directed
                    by William Gaskill, with Robert
                    Stephens, at the Royal Court.

April 1959   *The World of Paul Slickey*, directed
                    by John Osborne, with Dennis Lotis,
                    at the Pavilion, Bournemouth.
                    (Opened in the West End after a
                    tour.)

November 1960   *A Subject of Scandal and Concern*,
                    directed by Tony Richardson, with
                    Richard Burton, televised by the
                    BBC.

June 1961   *Luther*, directed by Tony Richardson, with Albert Finney, at the Theatre Royal, Nottingham. (Opened at the Royal Court after a tour.)

July 1962   *Plays for England*: *The Blood of the Bambergs*, directed by John Dexter, with John Meillon; *Under Plain Cover*, directed by Jonathan Miller, with Anton Rodgers and Ann Beach, at the Royal Court.

September 1964   *Inadmissible Evidence*, directed by Anthony Page, with Nicol Williamson, at the Royal Court.

June 1965   *A Patriot for Me*, directed by Anthony Page, with Maximilian Schell, at the Royal Court.

June 1966   *A Bond Honoured*, directed by John Dexter, with Robert Stephens, at the National Theatre.

May 1968   *Time Present*, directed by Anthony Page, with Jill Bennett, at the Royal Court.

July 1968   *The Hotel in Amsterdam*, directed by Anthony Page, with Paul Scofield, at the Royal Court. (Both plays transferred to the West End.)

August 1971   *West of Suez*, directed by Anthony Page, with Ralph Richardson and Jill Bennett, at the Royal Court.

CAST LISTS
OF LONDON PREMIERES

Look Back in Anger

Directed by Tony Richardson; designed by Alan Tagg.
Opened at the Royal Court Theatre on May 8, 1956.

Jimmy Porter	*Kenneth Haigh*
Cliff Lewis	*Alan Bates*
Alison Porter	*Mary Ure*
Helena Charles	*Helena Hughes*
Colonel Redfern	*John Welsh*

The Entertainer

Directed by Tony Richardson; designed by Alan Tagg;
costumes by Clare Jeffery; music by John Addison.
Opened at the Royal Court Theatre on April 10, 1957.

Billy Rice	*George Relph*
Jean Rice	*Dorothy Tutin*
Phoebe Rice	*Brenda de Banzie*
Archie Rice	*Laurence Olivier*
Frank Rice	*Richard Pasco*
Britannia	*Vivienne Drummond*
William Rice	*Aubrey Dexter*
Graham	*Stanley Meadows*

EPITAPH FOR GEORGE DILLON

Written in collaboration with Anthony Creighton. Directed by William Gaskill; designed by Stephen Doncaster. Opened at the Royal Court Theatre on February 11, 1958. The first English performance of the play was given by the Oxford Experimental Theatre Club at the Commercial Road Hall, Oxford, February 26, 1957.

Josie Elliot	*Wendy Craig*
Ruth Gray	*Yvonne Mitchell*
Mrs. Elliot	*Alison Leggatt*
Norah Elliot	*Avril Elgar*
Percy Elliot	*Toke Townley*
George Dillon	*Robert Stephens*
Geoffrey Colwyn-Stuart	*Philip Locke*
Mr. Webb	*Paul Bailey*
Barney Evans	*Nigel Davenport*

THE WORLD OF PAUL SLICKEY

Directed by John Osborne; designed by Hugh Casson; costumes by Jocelyn Rickards; music by Christopher Whelen; choreography by Kenneth Macmillan. Opened at the Palace Theatre on May 5, 1959.

Copy-Boys	*David Harding*
	Julian Bolt
Telephonist	*Norma Dunbar*
Jo, the Secretary	*Irene Hamilton*
Jack Oakham, alias	
Paul Slickey	*Dennis Lotis*
Common Man	*Ken Robson*
First Naval Man	*Ben Aris*
Second Naval Man	*Geoffrey Webb*
Deirdre Rawley	*Maureen Quinney*
Lady Mortlake	*Marie Löhr*
Trewin	*Aidan Turner*
Michael Rawley	*Jack Watling*
Mrs. Giltedge-Whyte	*Janet Hamilton-Smith*

Gillian Giltedge-Whyte	*Janet Gray*
Lord Mortlake	*Harry Welchman*
Schoolgirls	*Pamela Miller*
	Patricia Ashworth
Guide and Journalist	*Geoffrey Webb*
Photographer	*Charles Schuller*
Wendover	*Ben Aris*
George	*Tony Sympson*
Lesley Oakham	*Adrienne Corri*
Father Evilgreene	*Philip Locke*
Edna Francis-Evans	*Jane Shore*
Cornelia Tuesday	*Anna Sharkey*
Belgravia Lumley	*Patricia Ashworth*
Ida Merrick	*Stella Claire*
Terry Maroon	*Roy Sone*

Chorus of Journalists: *Geoffrey Webb, Ben Aris, Julian Bolt, David Harding, Ken Robson* and *Charles Schuller. Stella Claire, Patricia Ashworth, Norma Dunbar, Pamela Miller, Anna Sharkey* and *Jane Shore.*

A SUBJECT OF SCANDAL
AND CONCERN

Directed by Tony Richardson; designed by Tony Abbott. Broadcast by BBC Television on November 6, 1960.

The Narrator	*John Freeman*
George Holyoake	*Richard Burton*
Mrs. Holyoake	*Rachel Roberts*
Chairman	*George Howe*
Maitland	*Colin Douglas*
Mrs. Holyoake's Sister	*Hope Jackman*
Brother-in-Law	*Hamish Roughead*
Mr. Bubb	*Donald Eccles*
Chairman of the Magistrates	*Willoughby Goddard*
Captain Lefroy	*David C. Browning*
Mr. Pinching	*John Ruddock*
Captain Mason	*Ian Ainsley*

Mr. Cooper	*Robert Cawdron*
Mr. Jones	*Charles Carson*
Jailer	*John Dearth*
Clerk to the Assizes	*William Devlin*
Mr. Justice Erskine	*George Devine*
Mr. Alexander	*Nicholas Meredith*
Mr. Bartram	*Nigel Davenport*
Chaplain	*Andrew Keir*

LUTHER

Directed by Tony Richardson; designed by Jocelyn Herbert; music by John Addison. Opened at the Royal Court Theatre on July 27, 1961.

Knight	*Julian Glover*
Prior	*James Cairncross*
Martin	*Albert Finney*
Hans	*Bill Owen*
Lucas	*Peter Duguid*
Weinand	*Dan Meaden*
Tetzel	*Peter Bull*
Staupitz	*George Devine*
Cajetan	*John Moffatt*
Miltitz	*Robert Robinson*
Leo	*Charles Kay*
Eck	*James Cairncross*
Katherine	*Meryl Gourley*

Monks, Lords and Peasants: *Stacey Davies, Murray Evans, Derek Fuke* and *Malcolm Taylor*. Singers: *John Kirk, Ian Partridge, Frank Davies, Andrew Pearmain* and *David Read*. Children: *Roger Harbird* and *Paul Large*.

PLAYS FOR ENGLAND

The Blood of the Bambergs directed by John Dexter; *Under Plain Cover* directed by Jonathan Miller; both plays designed by Alan Tagg; music by John Addison. Opened at the Royal Court Theatre on July 19, 1962.

THE BLOOD OF THE BAMBERGS

Wimple	*James Cossins*
Cameraman	*John Maynard*
Lemon	*Billy Russell*
Floor Assistant	*Barbara Keogh*
Brown	*Glyn Owen*
Taft	*Graham Crowden*
Withers	*Anton Rodgers*
Guards	*Tony Caunter*
	Jimmy Gardner
Russell	*John Meillon*
First Footman	*Charles Lewsen*
Second Footman	*Norman Allen*
Third Footman	*John Maynard*
Woman	*Avril Elgar*
Melanie	*Vivian Pickles*
Archbishop	*Alan Bennett*
First Reporter	*Robin Chapman*
Second Reporter	*Barbara Keogh*
Third Reporter	*Tony Caunter*
Fourth Reporter	*Constance Lorne*
Fifth Reporter	*Jimmy Gardner*

UNDER PLAIN COVER

Postman	*Billy Russell*
Tim	*Anton Rodgers*
Jenny	*Ann Beach*
Stanley	*Glyn Owen*
First Reporter	*Robert Eastgate*
Second Reporter	*Donald Troesden*
Third Reporter	*Robin Chapman*
Fourth Reporter	*Tony Caunter*
Bridegroom's Mother	*Constance Lorne*
Bride's Mother	*Avril Elgar*
Bridegroom's Father	*James Cossins*
Bridegroom	*John Maynard*
Bridegroom's Brother	*Norman Allen*
Bride's Father	*Jimmy Gardner*
Waiter	*Charles Lewsen*
Guests	*Barbara Keogh*
	Pauline Taylor

INADMISSIBLE EVIDENCE

Directed by Anthony Page; designed by Jocelyn Herbert; sound by Marc Wilkinson. Opened at the Royal Court Theatre on September 9, 1964.

Jones	*John Quentin*
Bill Maitland	*Nicol Williamson*
Hudson	*Arthur Lowe*
Shirley	*Ann Beach*
Joy	*Lois Daine*
Mrs. Garnsey	*Clare Kelly*
Jane Maitland	*Natasha Pyne*
Liz	*Sheila Allen*

A PATRIOT FOR ME

Directed by Anthony Page; designed by Jocelyn Herbert; musical direction by Tibor Kunstler; lighting by Robert Ornbo. Opened at the Royal Court Theatre on June 30, 1965.

Alfred Redl	*Maximilian Schell*
August Siczynski	*John Castle*
Steinbauer	*Rio Fanning*
Ludwig Max von Kupfer	*Frederick Jaeger*
Kupfer's Seconds	*Lew Luton*
	Richard Morgan
Privates	*Tim Pearce*
	David Schurmann
	Thick Wilson
Lt. Col. Ludwig von Möhl	*Clive Morton*
Adjutant	*Timothy Carlton*
Maximilian von Taussig	*Edward Fox*
Albrecht	*Sandor Eles*
Waiters at Anna's	*Peter John*
	Domy Reiter
Whores	*Dona Martyn*
	Virginia Wetherell
	Jackie Daryl
	Sandra Hampton

Anna	*Laurel Mather*
Hilde	*Jennifer Jayne*
Stanitsin	*Desmond Perry*
Colonel Mischa Oblensky	*George Murcell*
General	
Conrad von Hotzendorf	*Sebastian Shaw*
Countess Sophia Delyanoff	*Jill Bennett*
Judge Advocate Jaroslav Kunz	*Ferdy Mayne*
Café Waiters	*Anthony Roye*
	Domy Reiter
Group at Table	*Dona Martyn*
	Laurel Mather
	Bryn Bartlett
	Cyril Wheeler
Young Man in Café	*Paul Robert*
Paul	*Douglas Sheldon*
Baron von Epp	*George Devine*
Ferdy	*John Forbes*
Figaro	*Thick Wilson*
Lieutenant Stefan Kovacs	*Hal Hamilton*
Marie-Antoinette	*Lew Luton*
Tsarina	*Domy Reiter*
Lady Godiva	*Peter John*
Flunkey	*David Schurmann*
Shepherdesses	*Franco Derosa*
	Robert Kidd
Dr. Schoepfer	*Vernon Dobtcheff*
Boy	*Franco Derosa*
Second Lieutenant	
Viktor Jerzabek	*Tim Pearce*
Hotel Waiters	*Bryn Bartlett*
	Lew Luton
Orderly	*Richard Morgan*
Mischa Lipschutz	*David Schurmann*
Mitzi Heigel	*Virginia Wetherell*
Minister	*Anthony Roye*
Voices of Deputies	*Clive Morton*
	Sebastian Shaw
	George Devine
	Vernon Dobtcheff
	Cyril Wheeler

Officers, Flunkeys, Hofburg Guests and Ball
Guests: *Timothy Carlton, Lew Luton, Hal Hamil-*

ton, Richard Morgan, John Forbes, Peter John, Cyril Wheeler, Douglas Sheldon, Bryn Bartlett, Dona Martyn, Virginia Wetherell, Jackie Daryl, Sandra Hampton, Laurel Mather, John Castle, Edward Fox, Paul Robert and Tim Pearce.

A Bond Honoured

Directed by John Dexter; designed by Michael Annals; lighting by Richard Pilbrow. Opened at the National Theatre on June 6, 1966.

Dionisio	*Michael Byrne*
Berlebeyo	*Graham Crowden*
Gerardo	*Paul Curran*
Lidora	*Janina Faye*
Tizon	*Gerald James*
Marcela	*Maggie Smith*
Leonido	*Robert Stephens*
Maid	*Chloe Ashcroft*
Zulema	*Neil Fitzpatrick*
Zarrabulli	*John Hallam*
Shepherd	*Frank Wylie*

Time Present

Directed by Anthony Page; designed by Tony Abbott and Donald Taylor; costumes by Ruth Myers; lighting by Andy Phillips. Opened at the Royal Court Theatre on May 23, 1968.

Edith	*Valerie Taylor*
Pauline	*Sarah Taunton*
Constance	*Katharine Blake*
Pamela	*Jill Bennett*
Murray	*Geoffrey Frederick*
Edward	*Tom Adams*
Abigail	*Kika Markham*
Bernard	*Harry Landis*

The Hotel in Amsterdam

Directed by Anthony Page; designed by Tony Abbott and Donald Taylor; costumes by Ruth Myers; lighting by Andy Phillips. Opened at the Royal Court Theatre on July 3, 1968.

Porter	*Anthony Douse*
Gus	*Joss Ackland*
Laurie	*Paul Scofield*
Margaret	*Isabel Dean*
Annie	*Judy Parfitt*
Amy	*Susan Engel*
Dan	*David Burke*
Waiter	*Ralph Watson*
Gillian	*Claire Davidson*

West of Suez

Directed by Anthony Page; settings by John Gunter; costumes by Ronald Patterson; lighting by Andy Phillips. Opened at the Royal Court on August 17, 1971.

Wyatt Gillman	*Ralph Richardson*
Robin	*Patricia Lawrence*
Frederica	*Jill Bennett*
Evangie	*Sheila Ballantine*
Mary	*Penelope Wilton*
Edward	*Geoffrey Palmer*
Robert	*Frank Wylie*
Patrick	*Willoughby Gray*
Christopher	*Nigel Hawthorne*
Alastair	*Anthony Gardner*
Owen Lamb	*Nicholas Selby*
Harry	*Peter Carlisle*
Mrs. James	*Sheila Burrell*
Leroi	*Raul Neunie*
Mr. Dekker	*John Bloomfield*
Mrs. Dekker	*Bessie Love*
Jed	*Jeffrey Shankley*
Islanders	*Leon Berton*
	Montgomery Matthew

CAST LISTS OF
NEW YORK PRODUCTIONS

LOOK BACK IN ANGER

Directed by Tony Richardson; setting by Alan Tagg; costumes by Motley; setting, lighting, and costumes supervised by Howard Bay; music for songs by Tom Eastwood; produced by David Merrick. Opened at the Lyceum Theatre on October 1, 1957.

Jimmy Porter	*Kenneth Haigh*
Cliff Lewis	*Alan Bates*
Alison Porter	*Mary Ure*
Helena Charles	*Vivienne Drummond*
Colonel Redfern	*Jack Livesey*

THE ENTERTAINER

Directed by Tony Richardson; settings by Alan Tagg; costumes by Clare Jeffrey; lighting and design supervision by Tharon Musser; musical direction by Gershon Kingsley; produced by David Merrick by special arrangement with The English Stage Company & L.O.P. Ltd. Opened at the Royal Theatre on February 12, 1958.

Billy Rice	*George Relph*
Jean Rice	*Joan Plowright*
Archie Rice	*Laurence Olivier*
Phoebe Rice	*Brenda de Banzie*
Frank Rice	*Richard Pasco*
Britannia	*Jeri Archer*
William Rice	*Guy Spaull*
Graham	*Peter Donat*

EPITAPH FOR GEORGE DILLON

Directed by William Gaskill; settings by Stephen Doncaster; supervised and lighted by Ralph Alswang; costumes supervised by Helene Pons; produced by David Merrick and Joshua Logan by arrangement with The English Stage Company. Opened at the John Golden Theatre on November 4, 1958.

Josie Elliot	*Wendy Craig*
Ruth Gray	*Eileen Herlie*
Mrs. Elliot	*Alison Leggatt*
Norah Elliot	*Avril Elgar*
Percy Elliot	*Frank Finlay*
George Dillon	*Robert Stephens*
Geoffrey Colwyn-Stuart	*James Valentine*
Mr. Webb	*David Vaughan*
Barney Evans	*Felix Deebank*

LUTHER

Directed by Tony Richardson; settings and costumes by Jocelyn Herbert; supervised by Thea Neu; music by John Addison; choral director Max Walmer; produced by David Merrick by arrangement with The English Stage Company and Oscar Lewenstein. Opened at the St. James Theatre on September 25, 1963.

Knight	*Glyn Owen*
Prior	*Ted Thurston*
Martin	*Albert Finney*
Hans	*Kenneth J. Warren*
Lucas	*Luis Van Rooten*

Reader	*Alfred Sandor*
Weinand	*John Heffernan*
Tetzel	*Peter Bull*
Staupitz	*Frank Shelley*
Cajetan	*John Moffatt*
Miltitz	*Robert Burr*
Leo	*Michael Egan*
Eck	*Martin Rudy*
Katherine	*Lorna Lewis*
Children	*Perry Golkin*
	Joseph Lamberta

Monks, lords, peasants: *Thor Arngrim, Harry Carlson, Stan Dworkin, Roger Hamilton, Konrad Matthaei, Alfred Sandor.*
Singers: *Paul Flores, Dan Goggin, Robert L. Hultman, Marvin Solley (soloist).*

INADMISSIBLE EVIDENCE

Directed by Anthony Page; settings and costumes by Jocelyn Herbert; lighting and design supervision by Lloyd Burlingame; produced by David Merrick Arts Foundation by arrangement with The English Stage Company. Opened at the Belasco Theatre on February 8, 1966.

Bill Maitland	*Nicol Williamson*
	(*James Patterson*, matinees)
Hudson	*Peter Sallis*
Jones	*Ted van Griethuysen*
Shirley	*Jeanne Hepple*
Joy	*Lois Daine*
Mrs. Garnsey	*Madeleine Sherwood*
Jane Maitland	*Jill Townsend*
Liz	*Valerie French*

A PATRIOT FOR ME

Directed by Peter Glenville; settings by Oliver Smith; costumes by Freddy Wittop; lighting by Thomas Skelton; music by Laurence Rosenthal; produced by the

David Merrick Arts Foundation. Opened at the Imperial
Theatre on October 5, 1969.

Alfred Redl	*Maximilian Schell*
August Siczynski	*Richard Jordan*
Steinbauer	*Tom V. V. Tammi*
Ludwig Max	
von Kupfer	*Jered Barclay*
Kupfer's Seconds	*Tom Lee Jones*
	Brian Sturdivant
Lt. Col.	
Ludwig von Mohl	*Staats Cotsworth*
Adjutant	*John Kramer*
Maximilian von	
Taussig	*Robert Stattel*
Albrecht	*John Horn*
Waiter at Anna's	*Bryan Young*
Hilde	*Mariclare Costello*
Whores	*Hedy Sontag*
	Marilyn Joseph
	Inge von Reith
	Billi Vitali
Anna	*Madlyn Cates*
Stanitsin	*James Dukas*
Col. Mischa Oblensky	*Keene Curtis*
Gen. Conrad	
von Hotzendorf	*Stefan Schnabel*
Countess	
Sophia Delyanoff	*Salome Jens*
Judge Advocate	
Jaroslav Kunz	*Ed Zimmermann*
Flunkeys	*Michael Goodwin*
	Christopher Pennock
Young Man in Cafe	*Warren Burton*
Passersby	*Eugene Stuckmann*
	Marilyn Joseph
Paul	*Christopher Pennock*
Privates	*Tom Lee Jones*
	John Kramer
	Brian Sturdivant
Ferdy	*Alan Brasington*
Salome	*Peter Colly*
Baron von Epp	*Dennis King*
Lt. Stefan Kovacs	*Michael Goodwin*

Tsarina	*Bryan Young*
Lady of Fashion	*Warren Burton*
Marie Antoinette	*Carl Jessop*
Orthodox Priest	*Tom Lee Jones*
Little Boy	*John Kramer*
Little Girl	*Christopher Pennock*
Equestrienne	*Eugene Stuckmann*
Balkan Chief	*Brian Sturdivant*
Shepherdesses	*Noel Craig*
	Luis Lopez-Cepero
	Peter Bartlett
Boy	*Tom Lee Jones*
2nd Lt.	
Victor Jerzabek	*Noel Craig*
Hotel Head Waiter	*Eugene Stuckmann*
Hotel Waiter	*Luis Lopez-Cepero*

Officers: *Peter Bartlett, Warren Burton, Noel Craig, Carl Jessop, Tom Lee Jones, Brian Sturdivant.*

Hofburg Guests: *Peter Bartlett, Alan Brasington, Warren Burton, Madlyn Cates, Luis Lopez-Ceperg, Peter Colly, Noel Craig, Carl Jessop, Tom Lee Jones, Marilyn Joseph, John Kramer, Hedy Sontag, Eugene Stuckmann, Brian Sturdivant, Billi Vitali, Inge Von Reith, Bryan Young.*

Musicians: *Frederic Hand, James Carter, Eric Lewis, Ruben Rivera.*

BIBLIOGRAPHY

PLAYS

A Bond Honoured. London: Faber and Faber, 1966.
The Entertainer. New York: Criterion Books, 1958.
Epitaph for George Dillon (in collaboration with Anthony Creighton). New York: Criterion Books, 1958.
Inadmissible Evidence. New York: Grove Press, 1965.
Look Back in Anger. New York: S. G. Phillips, 1957.
Luther. New York: Criterion Books, 1962.
A Patriot for Me. London: Faber and Faber, 1966.
Plays for England (*The Blood of the Bambergs* and *Under Plain Cover*); *The World of Paul Slickey*. New York: Grove Press, 1966.
A Subject of Scandal and Concern. London: Faber and Faber, 1961.
Time Present; *The Hotel in Amsterdam*. London: Faber and Faber, 1968.
The Right Prospectus. London: Faber and Faber, 1970.
Very Like a Whale. London: Faber and Faber, 1971.

SELECTED CRITICISM

Allsop, Kenneth. *The Angry Decade*. London: Peter Owen, 1958.
Armstrong, William A., ed. *Experimental Drama*. London: G. Bell and Sons, 1963.

Banham, Martin. *Osborne*. Edinburgh: Oliver and Boyd, 1969.

Brown, John Russell, ed. *Modern British Dramatists: A Collection of Critical Essays*. Englewood Cliffs, N.J.: Prentice-Hall, 1968.

Carter, Alan. *John Osborne*. Edinburgh: Oliver and Boyd, 1969.

Faber, M. D. "The Character of Jimmy Porter: An Approach to *Look Back in Anger*." *Modern Drama* 13 (May 1970): 67–77.

Gersh, Gabriel. "The Theatre of John Osborne." *Modern Drama* 10 (September 1967): 137–43.

Huss, Roy. "John Osborne's Backward Half-way Look." *Modern Drama* 6 (May 1963): 20–25.

Karrfalt, David H. "The Social Theme in Osborne's Plays." *Modern Drama* 13 (May 1970): 78–82.

Kitchin, Laurence. *Mid-century Drama*. London: Faber and Faber, 1960.

———. *Drama in the Sixties: Form and Interpretation*. London: Faber and Faber, 1966.

Taylor, John Russell. *Anger and After*. Baltimore: Penguin Books, 1963.

Trussler, Simon. *The Plays of John Osborne*. London: Gollancz, 1969.

INDEX